"I have come to believe that the insanity you are raised in becomes a part of you. In order to get the insanity completely out, you must equal it in your life so that you can get rid of it and move on. You don't get two cups of insanity and get to take only one cup out. At least I didn't. It's a terrifying thing to live through, and a blissful thing to be out of.

"When you are a child of abuse and no one listens to you and no one confirms that you are being abused, you feel like you are insane. The more you are denied your reality, the more insane you get. I am a child of abuse. . . ."

—Anne Heche, in *Call Me Crazy*

•   •   •

"[S]oul-baring . . . heartbreaking, often shocking."
—*Us Weekly*

CALL ME CRAZY

.

ANNE HECHE

WASHINGTON SQUARE PRESS

New York   London   Toronto   Sydney   Singapore

ISBN: 0-7434-2441-7

First Washington Square Press trade paperback printing March 2003

10 9 8 7 6 5 4 3 2 1

 WASHINGTON SQUARE PRESS and colophon are
registered trademarks of Simon & Schuster, Inc.

For information regarding special discounts for bulk purchases,
please contact Simon & Schuster Special Sales at 1-800-456-6798
or business@simonandschuster.com

Printed in the U.S.A.

The names of some individuals have been changed.

Owing to limitations of space, song credits appear on page 251.

For Kathy, Lauren, and Harley,
who brought me to the other side,
and for Coley,
who was waiting for me there

CALL ME CRAZY

PROLOGUE

I stood at the top of the staircase. It was old, more than a hundred years, I was told when we moved there. It was white as I remember and the railing unsturdy even for a child of six to hold on to. But I didn't hold. I stood, always in a white summery nightgown that had been passed down by my sister or cousin and was probably hand-sewn with a ruffle around the bottom. My breath was silent as I inhaled, closed my eyes, held out my arms, and leapt. I landed on the stair beneath the top, but I landed on my toes. I had floated, from one step to another. But I wasn't satisfied. I marched up that one step to the top and began again. A breath, eyes closed, arms out and . . . go. Three steps down this time. No trouble, no pain. Sweet. Bliss. A loss of my tiny body held by the air as I floated. I asked myself if it could be real, if it were true. Was this really happening to me? I climbed three steps back to the top and decided to dive in. My breath was stronger on the inhale, my eyes closed tighter with the agony of this needing to be true, my arms powerful in their angelic pose, up and out to the sides. And then I leapt. With all my might. Up, up, and away. Weightless. Free abandon. It wasn't that long of a ride, but long enough. As I felt the landing at the bottom coming toward me, I easily touched down. Toe by toe until I was on solid ground again. Would anyone ever believe that I could actually fly?

FOREWORD

Call Me Crazy is the story of my life, told from childhood up until a certain day approximately two years ago when I understood, accepted and digested the truth about myself. I was sexually abused from infancy. I created another world and another personality to survive this abuse. On that day I chose to say good-bye to that delusion and live completely in reality for what would be the first time in my life. I live now, with my husband and baby, as a fully free individual. My abuse is not something I ignore or lie about any longer. I do not live in the shame of it, nor am I glad it happened to me. I am glad, however, that I have come to terms with it and accepted it as a part of me. My hope is that this book helps others do the same.

One out of every six girls and one out of every ten boys in the world are sexually abused by the time they are eighteen years old. One in ten of those children ever admit to it. Over eighty percent of the perpetrators are either relatives of those children or trusted family acquaintances. I have learned these statistics only this year. I have also learned that splitting off from yourself when you have been a victim of abuse is not unusual.

When I wrote my book I was telling my story with none of this information. I did no research. I did not want to be influenced by anyone else's story. To know now that I am not alone makes this book all the more important to me. When I finally stopped living in the shame of my abuse, I wanted to scream it from a mountaintop. I wanted everyone to know what I had done and how I had done it. Nothing was ever going to stand in the way of my truth again. My mountaintop was a *20/20* interview with Barbara Walters, and my book is the truth.

There are adults in this world who believe that it is their right to walk into the rooms of children, theirs or others, and fondle, touch, talk dirty, glance sensually, tease, flirt, slap, hit, punch, go down on, force themselves onto, into and/or rape them. We live in a world where priests are getting arrested for inappropriate conduct, abuse and rape of children. We hear on the news every day of another abduction, another child being sexualized, tortured and/or killed. And yet, when a child speaks out about what has happened, we often call them crazy, say they are lying, or tell them to shut up.

My story is my offering to the pool of consciousness that is developing right now around abuse. I believe that each story adds to the body of knowledge that encourages truth for those who are keeping secrets, and creates awareness for those not exposed to the problem. My belief is that healing is possible for every child of abuse. By healing I mean living fully as a free, healthy and loved human being without shame of the past. It takes work. Work and commitment. To yourself. To the child that was treated with disrespect. To the person that deserves love the most in your life— you.

CONTENTS

CONTENTS

PART ONE

·

BECOMING ANNE

CHAPTER ONE

·

THE GREAT ESCAPE

I ran away at two and a half. I only found out—or I should say remembered—this fact of my life after many years of therapy and rebirths and any other measure I could take to get myself up and out of the insanity I was living in until . . . well, until not so long ago. I'm now thirty-one, turning thirty-two on May 25. I'm a Gemini, but it was not my birth sign that made me the way I was. I wasn't born with it either. I had to learn to be crazy.

"Mom?" I said into the phone while sitting at my kitchen table years after I ran. I was in my midtwenties and feeling heartsick over having to forgive her again. I had already done it so many times. "Mom?"

"Hi, honey!"

She spoke in an octave that made me cringe. The tone of her voice had raised over the years with guilt, I imagine. The closer I got to the truth, the higher the octave got in her voice.

"Just so you know, before I tell you what I'm about to tell you, I don't blame you for any of it."

I thought I heard a high-octave squeak on the other end of the line, but that may have been a projection or a mouse in the wall. I didn't have mice.

Squeak!

I had chewed off the already-chewed nails on my fingers and they were most likely starting to bleed. I had a "problem," which she used to scold me for.

"Nail biting is *not* a very ladylike thing to do, Anne. It's unattractive."

I always wondered why people didn't look beyond the spotted bloody clumps to think that there was something hidden there, perhaps family secrets, perhaps pain.

Squeak!

"Are you biting your nails, young lady?"

"Of course not, Mom. You heard me, right? I don't blame you for any of this?"

"Any of what, honey?"

Squeak!

I was beginning to think I had made the wrong decision by picking up the phone. Maybe I needed eight more years of therapy before I could make this call.

"Well—" I stammered, "I want to ask you a couple of questions about my childhood."

Squeak!

This was not a subject we liked to talk about and it usually led to a fight.

"As you know, I don't really remember much, but I'll tell you what I do."

"Great. Thanks. That's all I want. Did I say I already forgive you for everything and I don't blame you?"

"What was that, honey?"

I thought she had probably put down the phone to check her hair or look out the window or anything to avoid what I was about to ask.

"Did I by any chance . . ." Oh, God. All of a sudden all over my body I had the creepy feeling that everything I had spent the last eight years remembering was a lie. I had heard rumors that kids had been influenced by their therapists to remember bad things so that they stayed in therapy longer and hated their parents and attached to the people they paid to listen to their problems. Anyway, if I was crazy and had remembered all wrong, she wouldn't confirm my first memory. "Did I . . . ever . . . run away?"

Squeak!

"Run away?"

I couldn't stop now. The words were already out of my mouth. "When I was two and a half. There was a fire in the house when I got home or when I was found. Was there a fire? Was I gone? Do you remember?"

Squeak!

We had lived in a town house in a place in Ohio that I remembered as Something-or-other Heights but could remember nothing else about it. When I mentioned it to other people throughout my life, some would suggest, "Cedar Heights?" or "Shaker Heights?" I decided it was Shaker Heights. We were very religious and I connected religion with the Shakers. I don't even know if the Shakers are religious, but they sure have nice furniture. Shaker Heights was also supposedly a very nice area of Ohio outside Cleveland, and I knew that my parents always liked to say that we lived someplace that was expensive to the ear.

"Oh, honey!"

I thought my eardrums would burst.

Squeak!

"How on earth do you remember that? I haven't thought of that in ages."

When she said ages I thought of a song my mother used to

always sing around the house. *Rock of ages, cleft for me . . . let me hide myself in thee . . .* I never did know what cleft meant, but we were the absolute best at hiding behind or in anything, especially Jesus or Jesus' rock or just simply behind a rock—any rock.

"So I did?"

I couldn't believe it. If this was true, then most likely it would all be true. The running away was the most obscure of memories and the oldest. "So it's true? The running away and the fire?"

Squeak!

"Well, I don't know if I would have called it running away. You were missing," she clarified.

"And the fire? Was there a fire by the time I showed up again?"

"There was a fire that day. Yes, I remember a fire. What's this about?"

We lived in a row of town houses as I remembered it. Ours was at one end. I had snuck out and down the row to another two-story structure where a friend or playmate of mine lived. I don't remember what I was feeling as I did it. I don't recall if I walked or crawled or if I was crying or screaming or if I had already learned that that got me nowhere. By the time I returned, or was brought home or found, who knows which, the house was burning down.

"Dad set that fire, Mom."

She would want to put the phone down again. She would want the call to have been about a role I had gotten, or a boy I was seeing or a piece of furniture I had found at a swap meet or a new lipstick color . . .

"I wouldn't be surprised by anything your father did at this point. How do you know?" She couldn't help but ask. Her fear and curiosity blended in a scorching aroma. Her daughter was asking yes-or-no questions that she didn't want to answer. She knew that I had had little memory of my childhood in the past and that things had clearly changed.

"I know a lot of things." She had already admitted years earlier that I always knew things before anyone else in the family.

"Why did you remember this, Anne?"

The town house burned down. Or at least it burned enough that we would have to move. Why did he do it? This man? This father? There could have been so many reasons. The thing each had in common was that he wanted to hide. Which thing in particular on this day probably even he didn't know. I was learning to talk. He didn't have any money.

Insurance companies bought his lies because there was no reason not to. He was the choir director of a church he had started with another man who was the preacher. He was blond-haired and blue-eyed and fair-skinned and certainly looked the part of a man who would tell the truth. He was dynamic and charming and everyone liked him.

We packed our charred belongings and moved on, away from what we didn't want to know and didn't take the time to discover. This would be the pattern of our lives until he died.

CHAPTER TWO

CENTURIES OF MEMORIES

The house we moved into was absolutely stunning. It would be the house I referred to as home for the rest of my childhood. Who knew that insurance would pay for a bigger and better home, or maybe Dad's parents paid for it or my mother's parents—we were never clued in. We just went where we were told, and this place was a beauty. It was a "century home." We were enlightened to this like it was a prize or present that we would keep on opening. More than one hundred years old, it sat on the side of a long stone driveway away from the road and shone white and lovely with accents of black shutters. As far as I can remember, everyone loved it. By everyone, I mean the family. I was not an only child. There were four of us children. Four that were alive. We had one sister, Cynthia was her name, who had died years before. We never spoke of her except to say: "There are four children in our family and a sister who died and is in heaven with Jesus."

I loved that I had another sister. I used to fantasize that I would go to heaven and meet her. "When I go to heaven I'm going to meet her and we'll be friends," I would say with a smile to everyone I met, like it was a good thing that she was dead. It gave me something to look forward to.

That's all there was to say or think about Cynthia. We never knew why or when she died. We weren't told. We didn't speak of unpleasant things in our family, and the number-one rule was never to ask questions. We learned this rule by getting hit with a wooden spoon on our bare asses if we did. We didn't know of war or famine or Nazis or blacks or Jews. All of these "things" would fall under the category of "unpleasant" for my family, so we children conveniently had the wool pulled over our eyes from the day we were born. We were a happy, white, Christian, blond-haired, blue-eyed family—*Squeak!*

Susan was the oldest. She was twelve years older than me and lived in the attic. We didn't see very much of her because she was always busy doing things that we little children didn't understand. And she was probably right. We didn't understand much. We didn't have a TV, we never saw movies—certainly they were works of the devil— and we never read books. The activity we were allowed to engage in was Bible-verse memorization. I'm sure Susan was called upon once or twice to run our lines with us before church, but other than that, she was the sister ghost who did interesting things in her attic and we didn't bug her about it. She was an artist. She did paintings and wrote poetry that none of us were allowed to read. In fact, her poetry was so unreadable that the church my father started burned it. Yes, that's right, my father found some of her poetry and it must have been so entirely scandalous that it was burned and she was told to never write poetry again. Her art became her outlet, her poetry ordeal an example for us all to keep our thoughts to ourselves.

Next in line was Nathan. Well, not really next. Cynthia was

born in between Susan and Nathan. Nathan is now seeing her in heaven. But when we moved into the century home, Nathan was five years older than I. He was the image of a big brother. I don't know what that really describes other than that he was a bully and did things that were naughty by nature. He would throw footballs in the house when he was under strict orders not to, he would wrestle his sisters when he was under strict orders not to, he would go outside when he was under strict orders not to . . . you get the point. He was strictly ordered not to do a lot of things, and did them anyway. Does this paint a picture of a boy wanting to get attention for something that he *was not allowed to be doing*? Hmmmm-mmm . . .

Abigail was the blond-haired beauty that everyone was in love with. Her eyes sparkled, her hair glistened, her smile lit up the world. She was two and a half years older than I was, and from what I hear, we were so close we couldn't be separated. She, in fact, skipped going to kindergarten to stay at home and play with me. Clearly this did not affect her brain. She would later skip the eleventh grade to graduate with Nathan so that they could attend college together. Although, as it turned out, that didn't happen, Abi was brains and beauty to behold. We shared a room in this century home, twin beds side by side. I think we would have shared secrets, but we were so strictly told to never open our mouths that secrets didn't escape.

Mom and Dad's room was right around the corner from ours and Nathan's was down the hall. There was a rickety old staircase that led downstairs. It was a comfortable house, with a living room, dining room, and kitchen. A beautiful back porch that led to the backyard where there was a hammock, an acre of land that we all used to brag about, and a tree house in the weeping willow down the drive next to the garage. By the looks of it everything was perfect—normal, exactly as designed. We looked and told ourselves that we were the perfect American family, and no one argued. Why would they?

We were members of the country club and of the church—just like other normal working families. Abi and Nathan were members of the swim team and won ribbons at all of the meets, where they would chug pink Jell-O sugar before they dove into the frosty waters. I was jealous. I wanted to do everything my older siblings did. They dove off the high dive at the pool and had friends that would give them the equivalent of high fives when they won. I really don't know if people gave high fives back then. It's a trend now that's so silly I can't believe we all do it, but we do. Whenever someone does something good it's "High five!" And we smack hands. Hilarious.

(Human behavior is so intriguing. I find myself giving thumbs-up signs all the time. I know I look like an absolute dork, but I do it anyway. I want to get a trend going where we're giving each other thumbs-up signs for just being alive and walking down the street. Sometimes life is so hard and we judge people rather than realizing that it's an accomplishment to simply get up in the morning. So . . . *thumbs-up*! You're awake.)

I was so anxious to learn what Abi and Nate were doing that one day I climbed to the top of the high dive. Once there, I realized that I was scared out of my mind. For some reason, my father was there, which was a rare occasion. He climbed up behind me and pushed me off—no warning. This was the subtlety of my father. Maybe he was right. After that I don't remember being scared of anything, at least not anything that I would admit publicly or in front of him. Someone at the club must have taken notice because soon after that I was asked to be a replacement on the swim team, and I was happily winning ribbons too. But the swim team didn't last.

I don't remember what happened first or last in the series of events that follow. The truth is I don't remember a whole lot about this time in my life or the years to come. My memories have come back sketchy to say the least—somehow our bodies and minds protect us from the whole truth—but I'll tell you what I know.

I remember getting a weird feeling when we were at the country club restaurant one night. We rarely went out to dinner, but we were there and Dad was talking to the maître d'. Talking turned to arguing and the next thing I knew, Dad was pocketing the wonderful-tasting butter mints that were sitting on the counter near the exit. I don't mean a couple of mints either—I'm talking the entire dish of mints. And then we were gone. Not only from the restaurant, but from the club altogether. We never swam in the pool or ate in the restaurant again.

I was in the middle of second grade by this point and Dad was disappearing rapidly from our lives. He was supposedly going to New York on business. His trips were getting more and more frequent the longer we stayed in the house. It was very curious to me, seeing that the only thing I had ever known my father to do was go out to the garage and look at the fabric samples he had collected. Yes, fabric samples. He had tons of them piled high in the garage out back. You know those books that you can flip through when you're trying to decide how to redecorate? Well, those books were littered by the hundreds all over the floor along with some carpet samples. Certainly this was strange for a man who didn't have a job, but his excuse was that he wanted to go into interior design and he knew some women who were helping him do just that. Well, Mom didn't say much to Dad about anything, but whenever he brought up those women or the whole interior decorating thing, you could tell she was upset. If I didn't know Christians better, I might have thought she hated those women.

Dad had dropped out of medical school when they were in college and Mom was pregnant with Susan, and although it wasn't mentioned often, you could hear her disappointment hidden in sentences like "Donald!" (Oh, yeah, that was his name.) "If you had only stayed in school and become a doctor we would have food to put on the table! How long do you think I can feed these children on five dollars a week!?"

Mom rarely spoke to my father that way. He would purse his lips like a prissy old woman with no sugar in her tea and stomp away with a condescending "Good Christian women respect their husbands! Don't ever say that to me again, Naaannncyyyy!!!"

Nancy was her name, and when he said it like that she shut up. I guess five dollars a week was what he got for playing piano on Sundays at our new church. That was the only job he seemed to keep. That and choir directing. He loved choir directing. He would sway his arms in the air like a fairy and everyone loved it, including my mother. He was good at music. Music and fabric samples. So when Dad told Mom that he was going to New York on business and the business was gas and oil, you can imagine her surprise.

Gas and oil, that's what I said. Now how on earth could a choir director from Aurora, Ohio, who doesn't have any skills other than knowing what shade of pink complements what shade of black and which notes are played in the key of G find himself in the business of selling gas and oil? No one could figure. Especially not my mother. But this was a perfect time to exercise the number-one rule. *No questions asked* was also a rule my mother had to abide by, and it was followed quickly by her number-two rule: *Good Christian women believe anything that their husbands tell them no matter how absurd it may sound.* This worked out well for my father. God knows it was absurd! My mother was stuck with a houseful of kids on a few dollars a week while Dad went off to New York City on whose tab no one knew, to develop a business in gas and oil, which he knew nothing about and had never mentioned before in his life. We kids, of course, were kept in the dark about all of it. We dutifully did everything we were told and didn't question when Dad was out of town on business for weeks at a time, because we didn't want to get beaten with a spoon.

We also didn't question anything when we stepped outside to be driven to school one day and the car was gone. Just gone. No sign of it anywhere and nothing to be said about it. Dad was out of town, so we knew he hadn't run off with it, but it was all excused with Mom's cheery "I'm sure it's just some sort of mix-up."

Like good children we nodded our heads in agreement. "Sure it is, Mom. Just a little mixer-upper. No worries."

We trudged back inside and made bread. Homemade bread always made everyone feel better, and it was food that was cheap.

We sprinkled cinnamon and sugar on the buttered stuff and we had sandwiches for a whole week. Who knows how we got along without a car, that part escapes me.

When Dad didn't show up for three weeks, claiming that he was snowed in and the airports wouldn't let any planes out, I think my mother started to get suspicious. The weeks that he had been home the previous months, he would fly in on a Saturday night, tell the kids that they were singing in church the next morning for the congregation's entertainment, and fly out on Sunday night. He couldn't rehearse the choir he used to love so much, spending as little time at home as he did, so we had become the choir. Dad had taught us to sing on key and we looked cute up on stage in our homemade clothes, so . . . why not? We sang the same songs over and over, our version of a hymn in three-part (our fourth was off to college by now) harmony. And like a good Christian congregation, no one said a word. They, like good wives and good children, kept their mouths shut and looked like they were enjoying each phrase we sang as if it were the first time they had heard it. Like the story of Jesus turning water into wine, Christians can listen to anything over and over again and seem to stay interested.

When I mistakenly asked about this phenomenon one Sunday after church, I was given the lovely speech my mother so often gave as I pulled up my dress to expose my young rump: "You know I don't want to be doing this, honey." Then she smacked me raw and sent me upstairs, hoping I would once and for all learn the number-one rule.

"What will it take to get the question mark out of that child's brain?" she must have thought—never questioning that she too was questioning, and even though she didn't want me to see it, I saw it in her eyes.

• • •

Mom was a wounded woman. She did her chores dutifully. She mowed the lawn, kept the house clean, put food on the table, and always kept up the appearance that everything was fine. She had a beautiful and convincing smile. Although she did all of this, neither she nor I can remember one family dinner together. She can't remember ever asking how any of our days were, or sitting doing homework together, or watching any of us play. She can't remember what we did, any of us. There was one Christian radio show we were allowed to listen to. It was on at four o'clock in the afternoon and since it was the only recreation we were allowed to have, I remembered it. *Sailor Sam,* it was called. The stories centered around a Christian sailor, obviously, but after that I'm sunk with memory of it. Mom was too. She remembered that we listened, but not what it said. All she recalled doing, she told me, was sitting in her rocking chair reading her Bible and wondering how she was going to feed her children on five dollars a week. Can you image that life? Sometimes I talk to her and feel so lonely for that woman, that mother. She's much different now, but I still feel the loneliness in her for what she never had and wanted so much.

One day Mom was out mowing the lawn and she sliced off her toe. I heard her screaming in the yard and came running out, trailed by Nate and Abi. We all burst into tears, thinking that she was going to die. Nothing like this had ever happened in our family. No one had been sick; we hadn't even been to a doctor for shots. I don't know if it was religion or lack of money, but we did not go to the doctor—until now. She didn't die, or lose her toe, thank goodness, but that was the only exposure I had had to doctors until the next bizarre Dad occurrence.

"Hepatitis?" My mother was stunned, confused. "What in the world . . . ? What's that?"

"It's something you get from eating bad fish," Dad said.

"But we didn't have fish."

"Yes, we did."

"When? I don't remember eating fish."

"Well, your memory must be off, we had fish."

(I love when other people tell you that you're crazy.)

"We didn't have fish, Don. I would remember if I had fish."

"We *did,* but if you don't remember, that really isn't the point—we all have to get shots, that's the point."

"Shots? What do you mean? What do we all need shots for?"

He sighed his prissy sigh he liked to sigh to let her know in his unsubtle way how stupid she was. "Shots for the hepatitis, Nancy. I don't want to have to say it again."

"Well, I'm sorry, Don. You're going to have to explain it to me a little clearer. The children have never had any shots before. I don't understand why they have to get shots now because you ate some fish on a day that you can't even remember."

Sigh.

"Maybe I ate it in New York."

"So it wasn't with me. You said that you ate it with me."

"Does it matter who I ate it with? I ate it. With you. With whomever."

"Yes it matters because you said it was with me and now you're saying it's not and I still don't understand no matter who you ate it with why the children have to get shots!"

"Are you accusing me of lying?"

"What?"

"Are you calling me a liar, Naaancccyyyy? I don't like when you talk to me this way."

"I don't like when you don't tell me what's going on in your life and I have to guess."

"Who's making you guess anything? I just told you that I ate some fish that's all. Can we stop this conversation and call the doctor?"

"What doctor? We don't have a doctor, Don. We've never had a doctor."

"I have a doctor."

"Since when do you have a doctor? We can't afford a doctor. Have you been seeing a doctor?????"

"For the fish."

"What?"

"I saw a doctor for the fish." *Sigh.* Purse. *Sigh.*

(Isn't it amazing how the guilty can make you feel guilty?)

"HOW DO YOU THINK I KNOW ABOUT THE HEPATI-TIS?" he screamed, wondering why she didn't know what she couldn't know.

"I don't know, Don! *I just don't know!*" She sometimes imitated his sarcastic tone of voice back to him and it really pissed him off.

"Why should I tell you any of this when you can't even remember eating the fish!"

"I. Didn't. Eat. Fish."

"Yes. You. Did."

I'm sure he stormed off and I'm sure that that was not the exact conversation, but judging from the arguments I heard, it went something like that. My mother would be left alone feeling like an ass and he would sulk and roll his eyes after stomping away from an argument that was all his fault. Dad was never to blame. Anyway—we were off to the doctor to get our first shots so we didn't get the fish disease from Dad. They hurt and we all now had a little hepatitis. Yay for us.

• • •

"Mom?"

She could barely answer.

"Mom, you still there?"

"I'm here. Where could I have gone?"

I hated to think of all the places she had gone before, in reality or not, to avoid all the conversations about unpleasant things—and this was certainly unpleasant and getting more so.

I hadn't yet told her of the therapy sessions where I had remembered being gagged. When I would lie on the floor choking, unable to breathe. I hadn't told her what it felt like not to be able to scream out because I had no words yet.

"What did Cynthia die of, Mom?" For all these years I had not asked and she certainly, after all these years, didn't want to answer. She may have put it so far back that it didn't exist any longer. But what mother can forget how her child died? Her second child.

Her young daughter. Her baby girl that died before she could speak. Her daughter who was now in heaven because—

"She had a problem with her heart."

I'll say she did. Such a problem, she couldn't stick around to take it. Her heart couldn't handle my family. My heart was having a hard time too. It was beating out of my shirt. My heart was so far out of my shirt it was out the kitchen door, in the backyard where I had planted a tree. It was in the ground under the tree almost buried, unable to beat, unable to beat, unable to breathe. I felt so much like I had felt in those sessions when I remembered. The sessions when I wanted to die because something was happening to me to stop my breathing and it wasn't in my control and I couldn't scream because I was being suffocated and I wanted my mother to come in the door and stop it, but she never did. She never stopped it, and now I knew. One of my sisters was dead and I was alive, and I knew. I knew and my knowing was now making us both choke. I hated what I had to tell her, but I wasn't going to let him kill me. I was going to beat. I pulled my heart out of the ground and back into the house where I was sitting, and I committed to breathing. I committed to my life even if my sister didn't have hers.

I tried to hold back the blame, but I wanted to scream: *"You didn't save me! I was young, I couldn't speak! He had his dick in my mouth and you didn't save me, you bitch! She's dead and I'm not and you didn't save me. I wanted you to save me. Do you hear? Do you hear me now? Can you hear me now?"*

But I didn't dare. I was angry and sad and mad and all the things that I had been in the rooms with my therapists. I had done all the yelling, all the screaming. I had smashed my face into pillows, screaming where it was safe and no one would get defensive and no one would disappoint me. I had promised myself that I was ready for this conversation. That I could tell her without blame because she didn't know, even though down deep inside I didn't understand how she couldn't. How can a mother not know that her child—her young baby girl—is being raped by her husband? How can a mother not know? When does a mother break the rules?

"I have to tell you about Dad and what he did to me, Mom." I sat silently, waiting for her to respond.

"Did you hear me?" I asked calmly and with the hope that for once in my life she had.

"I heard you, Anne."

There was no emotion in her voice. I wondered if it had gone out in the yard and was under the tree where mine had been. I wondered if she had a yard and a tree and then I remembered that she lived in a very tall building and there were no trees and there was no yard.

"I heard you."

Just hearing those words made my heart return. It was the first time that my mother had acknowledged hearing me. I didn't know if she could comprehend what I was saying. I didn't know if her small body could bear what I was saying. She had lost one daughter and another was holding on by strings and a son was dead. Was this where the conversation was leading? Was it all going to become clear? Had the youngest daughter put all the pieces together and called her on the phone to tell her what she knew?

"What did he do, Anne?"

This was the question I didn't know if she would ask. I held my arms around myself as I felt the words drop from my mouth with my tears and into her ears.

"Dad sexually abused me, Mom."

• • •

There must have been a conversation, which of course we children weren't privy to. Children's opinions didn't matter and, besides, didn't we want to see more of our father? If he was going to be away all the time, we may as well move to where he went away to. I was in the middle of second grade, Abi and Nate were in the middle of their grades, but that was not a consideration. It was time to move to be near our father, and sooner than soon we were packing up all our belongings in liquor boxes found in the garbage behind the local grocery store. There was, however, some unfinished business, in my father's opinion.

Our church met in a college auditorium because they didn't have the money to build a proper church. Certainly the collection plates were filling with the tithe of all the followers. A tithe, if you don't know, is what each member of the church is supposed to give—or should I say *encouraged* to give—out of their paychecks each week. It is 10 percent of your salary if you want to go to heaven, or at least that's what you're led to believe. No matter how little money our family had, we always gave 10 percent. If we weren't members of a church, we would give it to Jim and Tammy. You know Jim and Tammy? The lady with all the makeup and the guy who was convicted of fraud? Those are the ones. We called up the number on the screen and gave and gave like the suckers that we were. My father must have thought that his measly 10 percent would save his soul or at least his car, but look where that went—the pound!

For years I thought I hated both of them, but then I saw a documentary on Tammy Faye Bakker and saw that she was so gracious, so ahead of her time. Even all that mascara didn't cloud her brain. She was the first Evangelical to have gay Christians on her show, and she single-mindedly preached love and acceptance for everyone. And she meant *everyone*—beautiful! I had no idea. That certainly wasn't the message that our parents encouraged. It made me feel better that I had donated my pennies to her, and I hoped that my money had gone to her and not her lying husband.

Anyway—this tithe thing seems like the greatest scam on the planet to me. Tell all the people sitting in the pews or the auditorium seats that in order for God to love you, you have to give him 10 percent. Who, him? I don't remember anywhere in the Bible, and I read a lot of it, where it says that God or Jesus or anybody requires 10 percent of your money to *prove* that you're a good person or that you abide by the Ten Commandments. Certainly my memory is cloudy, but God and Jesus are in heaven where the streets are paved with gold. If they need the money they can take a chip off the old block, no? There are crystal cathedrals and God-lovin' theme parks built on all these poor people's money, and they still tithe and tithe.

Where does it say that God needs a theme park again? The preachers tell you that *you'll* be rewarded while *they're* driving around in Bentleys and families like ours can't even feed their kids. Can no one see through this? Am I missing something? When do the congregations of these churches start to get back a percentage of the millions that the church is making? It doesn't seem fair that all they get is a ride on Jesus' roller coaster after they pay an admission fee for a park that they helped build! Oh, Lord. Someone stop me!

So our church met in a college auditorium, that's what I was saying, and my father had some unfinished business. That business was my baptism. Now, if you don't know what baptism is, I'll tell ya. There's a thing with "born-again Christians" (which is the correct title for what we were), where you have to accept Jesus Christ as your personal Lord and Savior. Now, what this means is that you must personally and in most cases publicly say a prayer that asks Jesus to come into your heart. I have been to so many of these ceremonies and they're all a little different, but most go something like this: The preacher gives an entire sermon about how everyone sitting in the congregation is a sinner. This is a hot topic for preachers and again is one of those things that Christians seem to be able to listen to over and over again. Clearly Christians are gluttons for punishment because in every sermon there seems to be at least one mention by the dude at the pulpit that "you are all sinners. Each and every one of you."

And then everyone nods their agreement like they've never heard it before and enjoy hearing even if they have. Some people get tears in their eyes, some sob, others just look guilty as all sin. Did I say sin? And what the heck is sin anyway? Aren't we here to learn lessons? Don't we all make mistakes, God forbid? God forbid is right. Mistakes are not allowed or you will burn in the fiery flames of hell for eternity—*unless!* Yes, there is an unless.

"Unless you accept the Lord Jesus Christ as your personal Lord and Savior. Can I hear an Amen!"

"Amen! Amen!" booms from the congregation with more enthusiasm than when their kids get straight-A report cards. It's really something to behold, seeing that most of the people have already accepted the Lord about a hundred times because they're afraid God might not have heard them the first, second, and third times they did it. What's worse is that the people who haven't done this one thing to keep themselves out of hell feel extremely guilty and are put on the spot by everyone around them staring at them like the terrible sinners that they are. The preacher continues by explaining that all the people who have not accepted Jesus can stand and walk to the front of the church where either he or one of the higher-ups in the church will pray with them so that they will no longer fall into the hands of the devil.

Without a doubt there are many guilty who stand and walk, sullen with their guilt, to the front of the church or chapel, or school auditorium in my case. I was six or six and a half when I walked this walk. I had no idea what I was doing, and it wasn't really explained to me other than that if I didn't do it, I was going to burn in hell. I certainly didn't take the time to point out or even believe that I was already in hell and certainly the devil would be more entertaining than the preacher. I, like the good little girl I was, didn't even think that there was anything wrong with this picture. I joined a whole bunch of other sinners at the foot of the pulpit and cried tears of—well, fear mostly—but tears of a six-year-old sinner. My tears and the others' tears were truly convincing, because before I knew it, a member of the church had her arms around me and I was being ushered to a bare spot on the floor and instructed to kneel down. I did, by golly. Nothing was going to stop me from not going to hell. As the tears rolled down my cheeks I heard, "What's your name, dear?"

They wanted to know my name? Didn't they already know? I sang in church all these Sundays and they didn't know my name? I wanted to say, "Hey, lady, are you crazy? I'm the girl whose father is the friggin' choir director. I stand up there almost every Sunday and sing my heart out for you. What do you mean, what's my name?"

"Anne," I said as sweet as I possibly could and then licked some tears off my lips, wondering why I was crying.

"Hello, Anne. You're making a big decision tonight."

These ceremonies always happened on Sunday nights as far as I could tell. I guess they didn't want to take up the time on Sunday mornings when the collection plates had to be passed. It was like they weighed the decision and decided fewer people would come at night so that's when they would recruit. Recruits were less important than money.

"I'm a sinner."

"Yes, you are, Anne. We all are."

I smiled sweetly again. I now had a friend who was a sinner too.

"Are you ready to accept the Lord Jesus Christ as your personal Savior tonight?"

"Yes, I am," I said. What else was I going to say? I had walked down the aisle with a bunch of other people and now the people who didn't walk were all staring at me. Yes, goddamnit, yes, I'm ready!

"Can you bow your head, Anne?" I could. Of course I could. I had learned how to bow my head before I learned how to say Mamma, for crying out loud. So I did.

"And repeat after me. Dear God in heaven . . ."

"Dear God in heaven . . ."

"I know that I am a sinner."

"I know that I am a sinner."

"I know that your son, Jesus Christ . . ."

"I know that your son, Jesus Christ . . ."

". . . died on the cross for my sins . . ."

". . . died on the cross for my sins . . ."

". . . so that I might be forgiven."

". . . so that I might be forgiven."

"Please come into my heart . . ."

"Please come into my heart . . ."

". . . and be my personal Lord and Savior."

". . . and be my personal Lord and Savior."

"Amen and Amen."

"Amen and Amen."

The woman gave me a big hug and I'll tell you what—I felt great!

I felt forgiven. For what I did not know, but I was forgiven and it was a good feeling. I was crying harder now, tears streaming down my face, a smile broad across my cheeks. I scanned the audience for my mom and dad and I'm sure I found them smiling back at me. I was a good kid, I really was. I did everything they asked, and now to top it all off I was forgiven for the things I had done and the things that I was going to do that I didn't know about that might be bad. Yippee! Let's dunk me!

The second step of this "Jesus-in-your-heart" process is the baptism. I had brought jeans and a T-shirt like my parents had instructed and filed into the bathroom with the other forgiven to change clothes and head to the indoor pool that was in the college down the hall from the auditorium. Abi joined me in the bathroom; she was going to get dunked too because when she accepted Jesus, the pool was closed or there was a swim meet happening or something. We sisters walked into the steamy, chlorinated room to see all the members of the church standing on the sides of the pool holding hands. In the water there was a line of sinners that hadn't been dunked, all in jeans and T-shirts, drenched up to their waists in water. The preacher and my father were holding two arms like in that game London Bridge when the bridge comes down, and the other two were held out to take the arms of the people being baptized. Once Dad and the preacher had a good grip on the person, they would dunk them back into their other arms that were clasped to give back support while underwater. The motion was quick and crisp. The person now fully dunked had all their sins washed away.

While I was waiting my turn I thought it would be really cool if we could see all of the sins floating in the pool like ghosts. I wanted to know what each of them had done, like stealing or having sex with their neighbor's wife. Of course, if the sins could have been seen, no one would be in that pool. Especially not my father. Can you imagine?

My turn! The water was coming up high on me, like around my neck. I was glad that I was such a good swimmer or I would be sunk.

I pulled my heavy clothes with me as I waded toward my father and the preacher and their bridge. I thought this was a strange game that adults played and wondered why they didn't think they looked silly like I thought they looked. I gathered my breath, looked my father in the eye, then the preacher, and before I knew it, I had water up my nose and was being told I was free. Free? Free of what? All my six-year-old sins? I don't know what I thought back then, I don't know what my little mind remembered or what ghosts I saw swimming into the deep end. I think I thought that I was a good daughter, a good Christian. I think I thought that I was doing the right thing and that my father would love me for it. I don't think I knew then that his form of love was bad or destructive or that I would spend years of my life trying to wash his sins off me. I'm quite sure I didn't know that I would be writing a book, like my own personal baptism, only wishing that the games he played with me had been as innocent as London Bridge.

> *I've been redeemed by the blood of the Lamb.*
> *Filled with the Holy Ghost I am.*
> *All my sins have washed away,*
> *I've been redeemed!*

CHAPTER THREE

MOVIN' UP

I didn't even know there was a thing called an ocean. That's how un-clued-in I was. I don't know if you blame that kind of thing on a parent, or on me not paying attention in school, but either way, I didn't know about it until we were flying over it.

"Oh, my goodness! What in the heck is that?" I might have asked, because God knows we did not curse. Cursing was an absolute no-no. I don't think I even knew curse words. Curse words, like the ocean, were things I was clueless about. We were not the kind of children who smoked cigarettes in the back woods and shared words like "shit" and "fuck" with each other. At least Abi and Nathan didn't with me. I was the youngest, however, and they might have done it behind my back. I was pure through and through, if you know what I mean. I gooed and gaaad over the things I was supposed to goo and gaa over. The ocean was one of them. I think it was in flight that we learned that although Dad had supposedly been working in New York City all these years, we were not moving there. We were moving to Atlantic City, New Jersey, instead. Neither one of these places meant anything to any of us, so we weren't disappointed like we would have been had we known the difference. Who the hell would have wanted to move to Atlantic City? There were no casinos yet—we got to see the Resorts Casino be built—and nothing else that would attract a family or anyone to this godforsaken place. Later I did discover a restaurant called White House Subs that's absolutely fantastic, and it's the only place I visit when I find myself back in AC.

Supposedly Dad had bought a house. I say supposedly because when we arrived, there was no house. There was a story of some weird old lady who hadn't moved out of the house that we were sup-posed to move into—but no house. We stayed at a strange apartment for a couple nights and then, like a miracle, were moving into a huge house by the beach on some fancy block that had a name we were told was on the Monopoly game. We didn't know what Monopoly was, but it sounded impressive, so we were impressed. We were impressed with a lot of things—especially things we didn't have and cost a lot of money or that people got attention for. We were all aware, whether we admitted it or not, that we were not rich. As a matter of fact, we were poor, plain and simple. But—and this is an important *but*—that didn't matter. We pretended we were rich.

It's not like we got lessons in this "pretend to be rich" game, we just followed suit with our parents. We wore clothes that looked rich. Even if it was one item that we wore all the time—we wore it everywhere and acted like we had fifty similar outfits in our closet. We went to expensive shops where we wouldn't buy anything, but liked that people were seeing us there. We combed our hair and brushed our teeth and smiled smiles that blond-haired, blue-eyed children should, and people believed that we were anything we said we were. Dad was the absolute master of this disastrous game. He pretended everything. He was poor and pretended he was rich.

He was bald and pretended he had hair. He was jobless and pretended he had a job. Oh, yeah, this was a kicker.

We arrived in Atlantic City and like a good family wanted to see where our daddy had been working all this time. He took us to an office where we met a very nice looking man named Oliver somebody, who distinctly wanted us nowhere near or around him. He was introduced to us as "my business partner, Oliver, everybody!"

We all smiled and responded with our best Christian "Hello, Oliver. So nice to meet you! So you're our daddy's business partner! Golly. Gee whiz!"

And in return we got a distinct *nothing*. As a matter of fact, one might have gotten the impression that Oliver didn't even know Daddy had a family at all. We stood awkwardly surrounded by what looked like office equipment, and I guess you could say that gas and oily–type things could have been done in there, but none of that really mattered because not two days after we arrived in this Atlantic City place with an ocean, Oliver and Daddy's business went bankrupt. That's right, folks. Who would have guessed that something our father knew nothing about wouldn't get off the ground? The most hilarious part of all of it was that we never questioned that Daddy had a business, we just played along with him and were totally bummed out that it went bankrupt. SUCKERS!

Unfortunately, this is not where the gas and oil conversation ended. Wouldn't you know that sooner than shit, Daddy was needing to go back to New York to do this gas and oil thingy. I'd say it took all of a week before Dad was off to the big city as frequently as he had been when we lived in Ohio, making promises in his wake.

"Yes, I know you all just moved here and I'm off again. But it won't be the same as it was last time. New York is just a hop, skip, and a jump away, and I'll be home much more than I was before. Isn't it you, Nannncccyyy, that's always complaining about having no money? Well, I'm going to make us money so that you don't have to be complaining anymore! Don't you know how much money there is to be made in *gas* and *oil*?"

So he was off and we hid our disappointment by quickly joining a church. Dad joined it too, and of course he became the choir director. We were now Methodists, whatever that meant. We were Baptists in the past and now we were Methodists, and nothing changed as far as I could tell. We went to Sunday school every Sunday morning and memorized more and more Bible verses, and when anything seemed wrong we would pray about it. Boy oh boy, did we ever pray! We prayed morning, noon, and night it seemed. We prayed for our father to get a job, we prayed for food on the table, we prayed for that weird old lady to move out of our house, and we prayed that Jesus would stay in our hearts. We were good little pray-ers. I even took my time at recess to pray. Pray and read the Bible.

Because I started school in the middle of the year, I felt really out of place. The teacher gave me a seat in the back of the room, and on my first day I realized that I was sunk. I looked up at the alphabet that was hanging on the top of the blackboard and didn't recognize it. I soon figured out that I had been taught something called ITA in my school in Aurora and it wasn't what they were teaching in Atlantic City. Supposedly what I was taught, something called Schwa, made you a terrific reader and speller. The only glitch was that you had to stay in that school system until the fourth grade to learn it all completely. Well, I was in the middle of second grade and wasn't about to admit that the real alphabet looked like French to me. I prayed that I would catch on sooner rather than later. Unfortunately, it was later. (Thank God for spell check—someone must have prayed really hard for that miracle, and I am eternally grateful.)

Eventually that weird old lady moved out of her house and we were moving in. This house was quite the opposite of our other one. It was situated on the main drag in a town called Ventnor; in fact, we lived on Ventnor Avenue. It was a big house with big rooms and each of us kids had our own bedroom. I guess we had made some money on our other house, because this house was bigger, and seemed to be more expensive. We set down roots. The kids were in school and Mom and Dad started a Bible study. Things were happy.

Because of our new religion, we could now celebrate Christmas in a tradition that we were not allowed to participate in in the past. So there *was* a difference—when you're a Baptist you don't have a tree and presents, but when you're a Methodist you do. I liked being a Methodist.

We bought a huge tree to put in the front hallway and, as we were new at this, had no idea how we were going to decorate it. Mom left these things up to Dad because, after all, he was going to be an interior designer before he decided on the gas and oil thing. Susan came home from college for the celebration and announced that her new name was Day. So Day and the kids waited with sweet anticipation for Dad to come home with the decorations. When the front door flew open, none was disappointed. Dad had a box of crystals from old chandeliers that he spilled onto the floor like a kid back from trick-or-treating with his candy. We were in awe. It looked like Dad had raided the largest diamond store in the world.

"What we're going to do is attach the ornament holders to the crystals and then I'm going to get some mirrors to hang along with the lights so that the whole tree glistens and reflects, and it will be the most heavenly vision of glass and mirrors that anyone has ever seen!"

Was that a lisp? Did anyone else hear a lisp? I swear he danced around the room and we all danced with him. It was the most extraordinary idea any of us had ever heard. And the vision! It would be magnificent to say the least. No one thought to ask where the crystals came from or how a man in the gas and oil industry comes up with such a sparkly idea. We just went along, hanging crystals and lights and mirrors wherever the wizard said they should go. It truly was the most incredible tree I had ever seen or have seen since. That was the thing about my father. He was a creative genius and we loved him for it.

• • •

Mom used to say that any of her children's creativity came from their father. When I was hating him, I hated hearing her say it, but it was true. Now she's said it enough times that I'm convinced. My father was a talent. He taught himself to play the piano when his parents told him that he wasn't allowed to play. He had to sneak sessions of alone time at the church organ and taught himself everything. He had the most extraordinary ear. You could hum a bar or phrase from a song and, before you knew it, his fingers would be dancing across the keys like he had been playing the song for years. What parents would tell their child that he couldn't play an instrument?

My father's father, although I don't know much about him (he was an "unpleasant" topic), was an alcoholic. He died before I was born and, from what I've heard, was not someone who was much missed. I think my father held secrets his whole life. I think he was beaten when his father didn't approve of him. I think he wanted to get out of the house and start a life on his own as soon as he could. At nineteen he attended a Christian camp where he was a lifeguard and met my mother. There is a picture of them together that I always remember loving that shows them standing by the pool in their old-fashioned swimsuits looking so young and innocent and hopeful. They got married that year in a little town in Indiana. They had both grown up there in different tiny towns, and I think they both wanted more than anything to get out of the households they were in and start one of their own.

I have come to believe that one of the most unfortunate things in this life is that you have to heal your own parental issues or you will, without a doubt, pass them on to your children. I don't think it's something that my mother or father was able to do—there was so much fear attached to being who they really wanted to be. I think there was a lack of encouragement to be oneself in that generation altogether. Women certainly weren't encouraged to be themselves; we can barely do that in society now. And sexuality? Who knew what that meant or how to express it? You were supposed to get married to have sex, and if you were raised in a Christian home, birth control was most likely out. My parents got married at nineteen and were giving birth at twenty. It was the first sex they had and—voilà!—they were having a baby. They weren't thinking about their issues. What were "issues"?

My mother's family was no fun ride either. She was born an identical twin and she and her sister competed their entire lives. They're still competing. I don't know if my grandmother truly loved her daughters—she certainly never showed it to my mother, and my mother suffered over that for years. Only now is my mother beginning to see that my sisters and I have the same arguments with her that she had with her mother. Her mother died recently without my mother ever feeling loved by her. My grandfather was a politician and again an "unpleasant," so I don't know much. I do know that he cheated on his wife, and after all the cheating that went on in my family, I know it affects the whole family unit, not just the one being cheated on. And then what did my mother do? She went out and married the most untrustworthy man there was. But she didn't know. She was in love and thought he was in love, and they didn't have pop psychology like we have now that at least warns us that we will meet our parents in each one of our relationships until we heal ourselves.

• • •

By the third grade I had decided that I wanted to be an astronaut, the president of the United States, or travel to Russia. I didn't know then that getting to Russia was not a career choice, but somewhere it must have sunk in that being president would get me there, so I wanted to be him. No mind that I was a girl. So, Russia or space—obviously I wanted to stay as close to home as possible. Mom was still under curiosity arrest, so she never asked why I wanted any of these things; she would simply nod her head if it was mentioned and go on making bread.

To update you on what I can remember, I had found a friend. A Jewish girl, the first one I had met—Jew, I mean—and I was fascinated because I had never heard that word before and quickly brought her home like a private show-and-tell.

"Mommy, Mommy! Look, I have a friend! She's Jewish and pretty." To me it was just another adjective that added to her interest. My mother was horrified. "What in the heck . . . ?" she might have expressed, if not for her plastered smile about everything until in private. And then when Amanda—Amanda was her name—left, it was, "What do you think you're doing, young lady? Do you know what she is? Do you have any idea?"

How could I? Why would I? She looked like a girl. Was I supposed to know anything else? She had dark hair and dark eyes and liked to play *Charlie's Angels*—whatever that was—and she held out her fingers in a gunlike fashion and I thought it was smart-looking when she did it. I thought everything Amanda did was smart. She dressed smart, looked smart, flirted with boys in a smartlike way.

"She's Jewish, Anne. Jewish."

"I know, Mom! That's what she told me too. Isn't she neat? Isn't she the neatest Jewish you ever saw?" What the heck was Jewish? "What the heck is Jewish anyway?"

Oops! A question slipped out. I knew that it must be something bad, something really, really bad, or she wouldn't be looking at me in that crosslike way. "We are born-agains, Anne Celeste. Jewish people are not. They do not believe what we believe."

I knew what was coming.

"They are sinners, Anne. Jews are sinners and sinners are Jews, and we don't associate with either because they are people of the devil."

Oh, my God. Oh, no. People of the devil? I didn't know what on earth Amanda and all her people did to deserve such fate as to not be associated with us and only be associated with the devil. I didn't know how many of the devil-people there were, but it sounded like a lot. Were they all the dark-haired people? Did she have a clan? Were they all young girls? Could boys be Jewish too? Were her parents Jewish? Something had to be done. Something simply had to be done. I liked Amanda. I didn't want her to be a Jewish devil-person. As fast as I could I rushed to her house on my bike, ran up the steps out of breath, and knocked vehemently on her door. I could barely wait till she got the door open to tell her.

"You're a sinner, Amanda, and you are of the devil. My mother just told me. You and all the Jewish people, and I don't know how many there are, but you have to be saved and it has to be fast or you'll go to hell when you die and be with the devil for eternity, and I don't want that because I like you. Please be saved. *Pleasssseeeeee!"*

Well, what eight-year-old girl in her right mind would say no? She wasn't about to want to burn in hell. Who would want that?

"What do I do? What on earth do I do?" She panicked.

Lucky for her we were still members of that Methodist church and they, like the Baptists, had a ceremony on Sunday nights to recruit all sinners to them. I took Amanda with my mother and my father the next Sunday night and sat next to Amanda, almost afraid to touch her, but glad she was going to repent for her evil Jewish ways.

When the preacher said, "You are all sinners. Each and every one of you," I hit Amanda on the leg and whispered, "That's you. You're the sinner."

She nodded her head in agreement and waited for the preacher to give her a chance to walk to the front like I told her he would do. When he asked for all the people in the audience who hadn't been saved to raise their hands, I nudged Amanda and her hand shot into the air. Before you knew it, Amanda and I were side by side (I went up with her for moral support) on our knees in front of the church, praying that Amanda would no longer be a bad sinning devil-Jew. The lady praying with her was very understanding and looked at me like I was a terrific Christian soldier for making my friend see the way, the truth, and the life. The congregation was on its feet, singing to the Lord and clapping their hands.

I am the resurrection (clap) *and the life* (clap clap clap clap).
He who believes in me shall never die.
I am the resurrection (clap) *and the life* (clap clap clap clap).
He who believes in me will live a new life.

Amanda and the others wept for their sins being taken away. I wept for her sins being taken away too. I wept and she wept and we hugged each other and wept some more. The Jew was no longer Jewish so I was allowed to be her friend again and nothing could make her or me happier.

"Can I hear an Amen?"

"Amen and Amen!"

I was so excited that I had changed someone from who they were into what I was that I decided that I was going to be a missionary and travel all over the world for no money, preaching the Gospel to every creature that would hear. I knew I could be convincing—look what I had done with Amanda, for crying out loud!

The next week I went with Amanda to a bar mitzvah where there was a beautiful ceremony in which a boy read from scriptures called something other than the Bible. After that there was a really cool party where everyone was dancing and singing and there was a tent with food and wine and everyone was having fun and laughing and the kid got a whole bunch of money. I thought to myself, "These sinning Jews sure do have a great time, and I don't see anyone that looks like the devil."

• • •

Dad had a new toupee on his head when he arrived back home after a very long stint in the city where we hadn't moved. He shared stories of grandeur with us like we would appreciate that he had been away having fabulous adventures without us and would surely like to listen.

"I drove Brooke Shields to school all week, kids. *Brooke Shields!* Can you believe it?"

We couldn't. Brooke was the incredible-looking Calvin Klein model at the time—the only reason we knew this was because Dad pulled pictures out of his breast pockets and passed them around for us all to gaze at so we knew who he was talking about. She was a stunner, all right! There was no doubting that, but how Dad knew her and what he was doing in a car with her was another issue. He told us she was soon coming out in a movie called *The Blue Lagoon,* which we wouldn't be allowed to see, but he was impressed and thought we should be impressed so we were most definitely impressed.

"You did? You drove Brooke Shields to school?"

"I did, I did. I just said I did, didn't I?"

"You did, you did. And we most certainly are impressed but ... In what did you drive her? What did you drive her in, Daddy? We haven't a car!"

Our car had yet again been repossessed one day while he was away and we were sure Dad hadn't bought a new one, and if he did, why weren't we driving in it and where was it parked? There were so many questions. So many goddamn questions that we weren't allowed to ask. He was driving a movie star to school and bragging about it and yet he couldn't make it to our school plays? Nathan and Abigail were both in a rendition of *The Wiz* at school and Dad couldn't make it, but he could drive a movie star to school. Was he saying that if we were in the movies, he would find time for us? Was that what he was trying to say? How were we supposed to be movie stars and when were we supposed to learn? We weren't allowed to watch movies, but we should be impressed by those who were in them? I didn't get it. Surely no one else got it either.

"How on earth do you know Brooke Shields?" I heard Mom ask.

"I'm best friends with her mother, Teri!" He said it like a cheer. Mom had never heard of his best friend Teri and neither had we. How long had he had a new best friend that none of us knew anything about and why hadn't we met her? This was all very confusing. And what, pray tell, did Teri have to do with gas and oil?

"Who is Teri and why have I not heard of her before? Does she have something to do with gas and oil? Are women involved in that kind of business?"

Sigh. Purse. *Sigh.* "No, she is not involved in gas and oil."

"Well, then, how do you know her? I thought you were away all this time on business. The business of gas and oil, Don. What business is *she* in?"

"You don't expect me to just sit at home after a hard day's work and not go out, do you, Naannnnccyyyy? I have to have friends. Don't tell me you expect me not to have any friends!?!"

I think she did expect that Dad didn't have friends. At least not friends that she didn't know about—at least not friends that took his time away from *his* children, from *his* family. If NYC was only a hop, skip, and a jump away, why didn't he jump on home to see Nathan and Abi in their school play and be proud of them instead of some tight-jeaned sexy chick named Brooke who was going to be in the movies we weren't allowed to see, instead of going out with this Teri lady? He obviously did not see things the way I saw them. So it hit me: In order for Dad to spend more time with his kids, we needed to be more than what we were. We needed to be different kinds of kids. We needed to do what *she* did. Immediately I decided that I needed to be Brooke in some form or fashion. If I couldn't have her looks, or a Calvin Klein jeans ad campaign, maybe I could be in the movies.

Would that be enough, Daddy? Would you love me then? Would you drive me to school and not somebody else? What could I do to make you love me the way that you love her, Daddy? . . . Daddy?

Wouldn't you know that about fifteen years later I had a movie called *Walking and Talking* at the Sundance Film Festival and I get a tap on my shoulder from who else but Brooke Shields? I couldn't believe it. I had taken Mom and Abi with me to celebrate and we all nearly dropped dead at the sight of her. She had become somewhat of a legend in my family history. There were so many times our father talked about her that we wondered if he remembered that he had children of his own.

"Oh, my God. Brooke! Brooke Shields!"

She smiled her lovely smile, which made me melt, and then said, "You were terrific. I was just at the screening, and you were great. I loved the movie."

"Oh, my God! You're telling me that *you* like *me*?" I had no idea how to speak to her or what to say. Here was a woman I had some-

how probably been in the movies because of, and she was compli-
menting me. I was beyond moved. I think I got tears in my eyes. I
think we all did. I threw my arms around her and choked out, "You
have no idea what this means to me to meet you."

She must have thought I was absolutely insane. Here was this
chick who she was simply telling that she liked a movie she was in,
and there were tears and hugs.

"Brooke . . . Brooke . . . before I explain why I'm being such an
absolute idiot, I want to introduce you to my mother and sister. This
is Abigail and Nancy, and you have been such a big part of our lives."
I'm sure she was flipping through her mental Rolodex of stalkers to
see if she had ever been stalked by three women before and what the
heck their names were and if they had been thrown in jail.

"We're huge fans, but we're more than that . . ." I'd better
explain quickly. We were standing in the middle of the street with
below-freezing temperatures and our feet were drenched in slush
and our tears frozen on our faces.

"I know this is going to sound crazy to you, but I've always
wanted to meet you and not just because I'm a fan and you're gorgeous . . . but . . . my father used to drive you to school, I think."

Brrrrr. Cold. Brrrrr.

She smiled her warm smile and was so gracious I just wanted to
kiss her. She could have smacked me across the face and walked
away based on how I was acting, but she looked at me with wonder and curiosity and said, "Really? You're kidding. Who's your
father?"

We stood on the street in the cold, me telling her what I knew,
Mom telling her what she knew, and Abi telling her what she
knew, and all it boiled down to was a collective "We really don't
know anything. He could have been lying. He was supposedly
friends with your mother. Your mother's name is Teri?"

It was. After a brief exchange on the people her mother used to
hang out with, it quickly added up in Brooke's mind. She was
hesitant to ask, but there was no other possibility. "Was he . . .
gay?"

He was. By this time we knew, even though we never found out from him. Dad had been dead for years now. Brooke's mother hung with the flamboyant crowd in New York in the late seventies and early eighties and, upon mentioning some other names, we resolved there on the street that Oliver, Dad's "business partner," had introduced Dad to Teri. It was the first and only thing we had really discovered that Dad didn't lie about regarding his travels to the city. He probably had driven her to school, although she couldn't specifically remember him.

It turned out that Brooke was in Sundance promoting a movie of her own, and she invited us all to the screening. We had dinner and wine and told stories and fell in like. She is one of the most wonderful people I have met. I sat next to her in the screening of her movie, beaming my adoration for her and my appreciation for how life works.

> *I wish I was a movie star*
> *It's what I'd like to be*
> *I'd work all day and never play*
> *It would be fun for me.*

I wrote that poem when I was eight years old, soon after our father told us about Brooke. If becoming a movie star was what it took to get my father to stop "playing" with me, then by golly I was going to do it. My mother sent that poem to me in a frame after I called her to tell her that I got the leading-lady role opposite Harrison Ford in the movie *Six Days Seven Nights*. She had kept it all those years but had never read between the lines.

• • •

"I had herpes, Mom. What eight-year-old girl has a sexually transmitted disease if she hasn't been having sex?" I was beginning to get frustrated.

"I didn't know you had herpes. How was I supposed to know?" She was beginning to get defensive.

54

"Because I came to you with growths on my face that were oozing and I didn't know what they were. Do you remember those growths on my face that you didn't do anything about and just said they would go away?"

"Oh, Anne. I know I didn't know much. I don't even think I knew what herpes was."

"Why didn't you take me to the doctor if you didn't know? Why didn't you do anything about it?"

"Did I say I didn't take you to the doctor?"

She hadn't said it. I just knew it. If she had taken me to the doctor, she would have known what it was. For years I had growths on my face and I was so embarrassed by them I never asked anybody what they were. My mother had ignored them my whole life, why shouldn't I?

"I guess that explains that terrible . . . diaper rash you had as a child."

"What diaper rash, Mom? I didn't know I had diaper rash. You never told me about a diaper rash."

Squeak!

"Oh, honey. They were . . . sores. I guess you could call them sores. It was so bad. You had such bad things on your vagina as a baby I couldn't . . . I couldn't put diapers on you. Oh, honey . . ."

Squeak! Squeak!

She was realizing things now at a rapid pace. Her emotion hadn't returned, and I was wondering why she wasn't saying that she was sorry.

"Why didn't you take me to the doctor? Why the fuck didn't you take me to the doctor?"

"Did I say I didn't take you to the doctor?"

"Well, did you? Did you take me?"

"I suppose I didn't. We didn't believe in doctors when you were a baby."

You didn't believe in doctors? Your baby has welts on her baby-size pussy and you can't put a diaper on her and you don't give a shit enough to trash your fucking beliefs for one goddamn second and take her to the doctor? Any doctor? Any-fucking-body who might tell you what was wrong with your baby girl's pussy?

It was all rushing through me. There were few things when I was a baby that my mother had told me about, but I was remembering them now. Now that she told me I had sores I remember her telling me that I had never had a bottle, never sucked a pacifier, never sucked my thumb. Never sucked. My mother told me that I only drank from a breast, a breast then right to a cup. Why was that, did she think? Why the fuck was that? It was a baby miracle I performed and no one ever knew why I didn't suck on the things babies normally suck on. I didn't suck and I didn't wear diapers.

Did it ever occur to you that I didn't want to suck on anything because I was forced to suck on things my whole life that I didn't want to be sucking on? Did anything ever occur to you? Did you ever think? Did you ever fucking think about anything that was going on right in front of your eyes? Right between your baby's legs? Right in your baby's mouth! Did you ever think?

"Oh, Anne . . . I was so much different then than I am now. I didn't think about anything back then."

Why was she not apologizing? I didn't understand. Here she was confirming all this stuff I had forced myself to look at so that I could get over hating myself, and she was taking absolutely no responsibility and wasn't even sorry, from what I could tell or hear. She must have moved to a place that had a tree. She must be under a tree in the ground. Her heart must be under a tree . . .

"Dad gave me herpes, Mom. I've had herpes my whole life and you're telling me now that you knew that I had a disease of some sort on my vagina and you did nothing about it."

"I was a different woman back then, Anne. A very different person." That's all she was going to give? *That's all she was going to say?* "Your father was a terrible, terrible man."

No shit, Sherlock! What was your first fucking clue? I wanted to spit in her face, hang up the phone, slit my wrists, kill her, kill myself—raise my father from the dead and kill him too. It would be better to be dead than be having this conversation alive. Did I say that she wasn't to blame? Did I say that I forgave her? I didn't forgive her anymore. I hated her. I hated her now more than ever. Goddamn did I hate her. But I couldn't turn back now. She was going to hear everything, because I was getting the feeling that I was never going to talk to her again. She was going to hear it all and have to sit with it for the rest of her life. She was going to know the whole truth and nothing but the truth so help her God.

*   *   *

Sing Hosanna! Sing Hosanna!
Sing Hosanna to the king of kings!
Everybody sing Hosanna! Sing Hosanna!
Sing Hosanna to the king!

Mom and Dad ran a Bible study at the house for twenty- to thirty-something couples in the church. No doubt they were the best example of a couple on the path of glory-to-God-in-the-highest that the church had to offer. Sometimes as a special treat they would have gatherings of fun-filled nights at the house when they would do things other than read the Bible and talk about their paths of right-eousness. On these special occasions, the children were sometimes allowed to participate—and, in one case, find her destiny.

Mom and Dad had taught us a "game" one happy time that was really a sketch called "Ah-ha! Wa-wa-wa!" Nathan, Abi, and I would all put on the most ridiculous hats and skirts we could find in the house and interact with each other by using only the sounds "Ah-ha!" and "Wa-wa-wa!" Depending on how the others said their line, you would have to respond with a reaction that comple-mented the way they had communicated to you. It was the first and simplest form of improvisation I learned and went something like this:

"Ah-ha!"
"Wa-wa-wa!"
"Ah-ha!"
"Waaaa-waaa-WA!"

"AAAAHHHHH—HAAAAA!"

"Wa-wa——wa!"

You get the point. Without a doubt the game would leave us all rolling in laughter. Sometimes Mom and Dad would join in the sketch, and it was the closest and most communicative our family got. When they realized what hams we all were, they were ready to show us off to the group.

The idea for this night was that each couple had to take a story from the Bible and act it out for the rest of the group. Then the group had to guess what story it was. Fun, right? So Mom and Dad told us about the game and said that we children could come up with a story of our own to start off the evening. Excitedly we put our heads together and came up with the story of "Jonah and the Whale."

Now, if you don't know this story, I'll fill you in. There's this dude—Jonah was his name—who was thrown off a fishing boat one day at sea. There were very choppy waters that particular afternoon and Jonah hit the waters hard! With all the waves and surf out in the middle of absolutely nowhere, it seemed like Jonah was going to drown. In fact, I think that was the intention of the guys that threw him off. (I'm sorry, I can't remember the reason he was tossed, but I think it was something about preaching the word of God. Or maybe he was just really annoying and didn't help clean the fish. Either way, these mean, nasty men didn't want him around, so tossed he was.) Now drenched and hurt and upset and confused, Jonah, being the godly man he was, looked to the heavens while treading water and choking and screamed something similar to what every other person in the Bible screams when in trouble: "My God! My God! Why hast thou forsaken me?" And next thing you know, a whale comes and swallows him up. No kidding. A whale swims to Jonah and swallows him up—whole! Once Jonah's safe inside, the big fish swims to shore and WHAMMY! Jonah is spit out—*whole and intact*—on the beach where he is safe and sound. The end.

After deciding which story we were going to do, the next step was casting the roles. Abi and Nathan decided that I should be Jonah because I was the smallest and the easiest to throw overboard. They would be the mean and nasty fisherman dudes. So we set out to make a boat. We carved boxes into the shape of a ship and drew fish along the sides and waves depicting the very choppy ocean. The plan was that after I was gently tossed overboard, Abi and Nate together would be the whale, Nate the jaws and Abi the tail. Once "swallowed up," I would get in the middle of both of them, we would wiggle like we were swimming to shore, and then they would jerk their bodies and I would shoot out of what looked to be Nathan's mouth.

When the time came, everyone gathered around our makeshift boat and oohed and aahed over how much work we had put into our sketch. I dressed up like a boy so that everyone knew that I was not a girl and did my best to look like Jonah-of-the-Bible-times. I don't know the exact dialogue, but this is close enough:

Nate: "Jonah, we don't like you!"

Abi: "Yeah, Jonah! You stink."

Nate: "A lot! We don't want you on our boat."

Abi: "We never really did. We don't know how you got here in the first place."

Anne: "God sent me."

Nate: "God? Enough about God!"

Abi: "Yeah. We don't like God and we don't like you."

Anne: "But God is the way, the truth, and the life! He who believes in him shall never die!"

Nate: "That's it! We've had it with you!"

Abi: "Yeah! You're dead!"

And with that Nathan and Abi grabbed my arms and feet, respectively, and started swinging me over the edge of the homemade boat.

Abi and Nate (swinging me in the air): "One . . . two . . ."

Anne: "No! Please, no!"

But before they got to three, I found my body careening over the cardboard boat and into the living room. Abi and Nathan got so into character that they let go of me while in midair and—*"Three!"*

I fell from about five feet up and landed flat on my back, smacking my head on the floor and really truly feeling what Jonah might have felt. "MY GOD! MY GOD! WHY HAST THOU FORSAKEN ME?" I screamed at the top of my lungs, everyone thinking that I was giving a fully committed Jonah-like performance. Abi and Nathan ran around the side of the boat and immediately became the whale. I couldn't stop the show now no matter how badly I was hurt. The whale was heading toward me and the crowd was most certainly riveted. I allowed myself to be swallowed up like we had planned. I grabbed my aching head once inside the belly and wiggled my tiny bottom like we had rehearsed.

"MY GOD!" I screamed. And Abi and Nathan echoed back, "MY GOOODDDD! MY GGGOOODDDDD!"

Before I knew it, Nathan was heaving and Abi was shooing and out I spilled. Regurgitated from the belly of the whale and out flat onto the floor, I was heaving and hurting and ready to cry.

As I watched Nathan and Abi swim away from our carpeted shore, I shakily got to my knees—

"My God!"

And then to my feet—

"My God!"

And raised my hands in the air—

"I'm alive! I'M ALIVE!"

And did a little jig.

"Thank you, God! Thank you!"

The entire Bible study got to their feet. My siblings ran to my sides and took my jiggy hands. As we were bending in our bow and I heard the cheers of my fans, my headache no longer mattered. My back pain went away. We took another bow, and I thought I heard my father turn to my mother and say, "A star is born."

I don't know if it was because of our performance or if it had nothing whatsoever to do with it, but soon after we were allowed to go to the theater to see our first movie. We were all so very excited.

There was a movie called *Star Wars* that was coming out starring this guy who used to be a carpenter and a pretty lady with buns on either side of her head. We decided to make an event out of the evening. There was a newfoundangled food we had learned about from our boardwalk excursions called "pizza-burgers" and Mom was going to make them for us before we went to the seven o'clock show. Dad had the job of making his very favorite and special recipe called "sugar popcorn." Sugar popcorn is made in oil and doused heavily in sugar and was one of our favorite treats. We were going to sneak it into the theater under our coats because we couldn't afford the tickets let alone the popcorn, but nothing was going to take away from the whole theater experience this night of nights.

We gobbled our gooey burgers, which consisted of chopped ham meat, mozzarella cheese, and tomato sauce, and were tumbling down the street as fast as you could say "Boo." We paid our money and skipped down the aisle, finding seats in the very first row. I could hardly bear all the excitement. The world on the screen was so wonderful, so fantastical. The men in white suits gave me the chills, the chick with the buns gave me the thrills, and the guy with the ship? Forget it. I mean forget it. Who the heck was that? What a dream. What a *dream*! I had never seen a man like him before. His face was so handsome, his ship so fine . . . I wanted to be on that ship. I wanted to boot that princess off and grow buns of my own. I wanted him to look at me the way he looked at her and fly me through space. Couldn't I fly with him? Couldn't I please, please, one day fly with him?

• • •

The fun, good-lovin' times were hard to come by in our house after that. My mother's father was dying and she spent most of her days crying. Dad was off all the time and our money was on a tight line. Nothing was coming in, which was something close to sin; the children were crabby, my herpes was scabby. We were all getting sick, the walls of denial so thick. It was bad and getting worse and things were stolen from Mom's purse; it was all crashing down, there was no smile only frown. It was all stinking bad and we were really really sad when—

"CHILDREN!!!!!!!!! WHERE ARE YOU!!!!!!!"

We heard Mom screaming from the top of the steps. The whole neighborhood could have heard her, she was yelling so loud. We most often did what we were told anyway, but this time we came rushing from wherever we were like bullets shooting from an AK-47.

"What, Mom? What? What's wrong?"

My mother was panting at the top of the steps, holding something that looked like a change purse in her hands.

"Who took it? Which one of you took it?"

We were all being accused of something, and her fury was so ugly we hoped that whoever it was would speak up and speak up fast. We looked at one another, searching for the thief. We searched and searched, and I knew it wasn't me, but whoever could it be . . .

"Who took the money?"

We were all shaking at the bottom of the steps. I could imagine that from my mother's point of view, we all looked so small and fragile now, shaking in our shoes.

"What money?" one of us asked, I don't know which one. We were all thinking the same thing at this point. What money? Who took the money? How much money was there? And, anyway, who knew where she kept it in order to take it?

"Answer me!"

Nobody answered.

"Nathan! Nathan Bradley!" Nathan was always the first to be blamed for bad things and his middle name was Bradley. Mom used it when she was extra peeved at him, and boy was she peeved. Like I said before, he did things he wasn't supposed to do, like throwing footballs in the house, but steal money? None of us had heard of him stealing anything! We looked at Nathan, and Nathan looked as shocked as us that he was the one being singled out.

"Mom, please, Mom. I did not take your money. I don't know

what you're talking about. I promise I have no idea." He sure sounded convincing, at least I was convinced, and I really wanted someone to be blamed so that Mom would feel relief and get that ugly sneering look off her face.

"I had four dollars in this purse. *Four dollars* and it's gone now. One of you took it, and I'm going to find out which one of you it was by the end of today if it kills me. Now, *who* did it?"

Jesus Christ, we were stumped. We were not bad enough kids to *not* admit this kind of thing. We hated seeing our mother like this. We wanted her to have the answer about where the four dollars had gone.

"This was our grocery money. *Our grocery money.* Do you kids understand?" We did, we did. We most definitely did understand. "How do you expect there to be food on the table if one of you is stealing the grocery money?"

I thought about trees and how money didn't grow on them.

"I'll have to ask your father what to do about this when he gets home." And with that she stomped off accusingly.

Abi and I turned to Nathan and whispered, "Did you take it?" We gobbled out the question over each other, wanting to know— needing to know. He whispered back, "No. No, I didn't take it. Did you?"

Abi and I looked shocked at the mere suggestion that we good little Christian girls would do such a thing. We both denied any involvement whatsoever as quickly as it could escape. "No! Of course not, no!" We were stumped.

"Who took it, then?" was the question, but the answer none of us knew.

Dad came home wearing a brand-new royal blue windbreaker that he showed off like a fur coat on the way to his bedroom. Mom quickly snagged him at the door and slammed it shut behind them. Within seconds we heard Mom yelling (she was beginning to not pay attention to the rules as much anymore) about where the hell he got it and what it was doing on his back. He yelled back some explanation about how he got it from one of Nathan's friends who was doing something or other for charity and was giving out slickers in return for a donation.

"A donation? Where on earth are you getting money for a charity donation?"

Surely Mother thought that we were the charity that Dad should be donating money to, and she was probably right.

"If you hadn't donated money to a charity, we could put food on the table, Don. Do you know that one of the kids stole the grocery money out of my purse and now we don't have any money for this week's food? That *charity* money could come in really handy about now! In fact, it would come in handy about a million other times before this and for much more important things than a slicker! I can't believe you thought it was okay to buy a slicker!"

Sigh. Purse. *Sigh.*

"It's not a slicker, it's a windbreaker, and who are you to tell me that I can't have a windbreaker if I want one? I don't have a windbreaker and I need a windbreaker!" *Sigh.* Purse.

"We don't have money for food, Don!"

"Well, it's not my fault that we don't have money for food. Who stole the money?"

"I don't know, that's what I've been saying. I asked them, but none of them confessed. What are we going to do about it? What do *you want* to do about it?"

"I can't believe that our kids are stealing money. Something has to be done."

"That's what I'm trying to tell you. Something has to be done. What are you going to do about it?"

There was quiet for a while while they contemplated what to do, and then the door flew open. They had come up with a solution and we were about to hear what it was.

"Kids! Get in here!" my father boomed like over the loudspeaker when someone gets called to the principal's office in school. We weren't about to do something other than what we were told at this particular moment. We all rushed into my parents' bedroom, which had blue and white frills left over from the weird lady who used to live there.

"Your mother just informed me that one of you took four dollars from her dresser this morning." Dresser? What dresser? Who said dresser? She told us that someone took it from her purse. We knew nothing of a dresser. No one had the balls to ask why he said *dresser,* and Mom didn't correct him. We assumed that the purse was in the dresser—the dresser in the corner that had a blue and white curtain around the bottom, where the weird lady would put on her makeup in the morning and that Mom was now standing by with her arms crossed.

"Now, I'm going to give you one chance and one chance only for you to admit which one of you took the money."

We three stood in silence, wondering what was going to happen after this one chance that he was giving us passed. Dad stared . . . and Mom stared . . . and the time of our chance was running out. After a few moments of staring, Mom nodded at Dad and Dad nodded at Mom and then she went to sit in a frilly chair next to the frilly dresser.

Sigh. Purse. *Sigh.* "That's it, then. If that's how you want it."

Dad went to his closet and pulled out a belt. He rarely used belts, but on this occasion, I suppose they decided that it was necessary to use something stronger than a wooden spoon. We were instructed to pull down our pants and lean over the bed one by one. The plan they had come up with was that Dad was going to hit us with the belt until one of us admitted to stealing the money. We would each get whacked three to five times—depending on what, we didn't know—and then have to stand and watch the others get hit until it was our turn again. I think Nathan was first in line because they thought he was guilty and would confess. Abi was next and then me.

We slowly pulled down our pants and held our breath as we leaned over the bed, one after another, time after time, hit after hit. The more times we leaned over, the harder the hits got. Nathan was trying so hard not to cry, not to scream out, but Abi and I couldn't help ourselves. We were bawling at each hit. I don't think I knew what hurt more—getting hit or watching my father hit Abi and Nathan. It was so painful, so dreadful. This circle of hitting and crying and smacking and wailing got so bad that finally I couldn't take it anymore. I lifted my head up from the bed and glared in my mother's direction. Her stoicism made it easier for me to choke out, "I think you stole it, Mom. I think you stole the money so that you could watch us get hit!"

Wham! That did *not* go over well. I was eight years old and accusing my mother of doing something that brought brutality to her children just so she could watch.

Wham! Wham! Wham!

(Why did I say that? What had she watched before? What gave me the thought that my mother would stand by and watch my father do something to me that hurt? Something that hurt so badly it made me scream in pain? How could a mother watch this brutality? How could she sit in that chair and not stop the cruelty?)

Wham! Wham! Wham!

"STOP! STOP IT!" I heard Nathan screaming out. "Stop it! I can't take it anymore. Just hit me, I don't care. Just keep hitting me. I didn't do it and I wish I did now, but I can't watch you hitting my sisters like this anymore. I'll take the blame. I'll take it, just keep hitting me!"

He threw his naked red rump on the bed beside me. It was all so ugly. I can't remember anything more ugly in my lifetime than this scene. We were all crying so hard. We all, but not my parents. My mother had venom for what I had said. My father had venom for my brother's heroics. I had venom for the whole goddamn scene. My father began pummeling Nathan again as hard as he could.

"You took it, Nathan. I know you took the money," he said as he whacked his belt down time and again.

Abi and I watched as the skin on Nathan's bottom reddened and split open. The lines from the belt were now drawn in blood, and still my father continued. Nathan could no longer hold back his tears, and he screamed out for my father to stop. I thought of when my mother told me that Jews were of the devil. I thought of when I saw the Jews and I knew that they weren't. She had been mistaken.

The devil was in our house, and he most certainly was *not* a Jew. He was a blond-haired, blue-eyed Christian. My father was the devil. I could see it now, see it in his eyes. They were red and furious, and the flames of hell were on my brother's innocent ass. I knew right then that my father had taken the money. My father had taken the money and bought the windbreaker and said it was for charity, but it wasn't for charity. My father didn't know from charity. He was the devil, and I saw it in his eyes.

It was only when the devil's arm got tired that he stopped hitting my brother.

Sigh. Pant. *Sigh*. Pant.

There was nothing more to say. Nothing more to do. Nathan shakily stumbled to his room, barely able to keep his legs beneath him—certainly unable to pull up his pants.

"God will punish you for this, Nathan! God will punish you!" The devil was seething at my brother. I wanted so badly to tell the devil to shut up. No God would do the damage he had done to us this day. No God I knew. I pulled up my pants and walked silently toward Nathan's room. I didn't know what I would say, but I wanted to thank him, tell him that he was my hero that day.

You saved my ass, I wish I could have said as he opened the door for me. But I couldn't get out any words. My brother was holding his can of quarters upside down, limp at his side. He had been collecting quarters all year and made a can in art class for the very purpose of it being a bank. Some days we would go into his room and pour the can onto his bed and count how many quarters he had saved. We would get excited with each new pile of four and sometimes play with them like they were soldiers—good Christian soldiers. But now there were none. No soldiers, no quarters. His soldiers had been stolen and there was nothing to be done.

• • •

When you are an abused child you are taught to be quiet. Sometimes you are threatened with your life, sometimes the threats are more subtle, but they are always ferocious and the child always knows. Sometimes the hurt is so bad that you can't talk about it even if you want to because it is too gruesome to describe. Sometimes you cry out and cry out and no one comes and no one hears so you can't tell. Sometimes you have a pillow shoved in your mouth or a sock or a fist or a cock so you can't scream out and you can't be heard and you can't believe it's happening so you can't say that it did when it finally stops. Sometimes you write it down to let someone know you're in trouble and they don't pay attention, so you write more and more and they ignore more and more, and soon you find your writing in the trash. Sometimes you come right out and say it and you are blatantly told that you are not telling the truth and to never bring it up again. Sometimes you tell and you get the shit beaten out of you so you don't tell again because you don't want to get beat after getting fucked. Sometimes you tell a neighbor or a friend of your parents or a friend's parents so that they will tell for you. Sometimes you tell your brother or sister and they don't want to believe you because it's too hard to believe and it's too hard to know what to do so they don't believe you or won't believe you. Sometimes there are so many lies and so much pain in the family that the truth has lost its meaning and nothing is true anymore. Sometimes you try everything in your power to convince *yourself* it's not true, but it keeps happening and no matter how much you keep on *not* believing, it happens some more and your belief loses its power. Sometimes you go absolutely crazy thinking that what *is* happening is *not* happening so you stop telling or trying because you've convinced yourself that *you do not know what you know.* Sometimes you don't know and you've given up trying because it doesn't matter anyway and it's easier to believe what *they* want you to believe. Sometimes you have a day when you believe you're okay and the thoughts will stay away, but you close your eyes at night and it gives you such a fright because nothing's gone away and your biggest fear is there to stay.

• • •

Somewhere amid the chaos of the quarters and the windbreakers we went back to being Baptists. The Methodists must not have agreed with Mom and Dad's form of punishment. Or maybe they didn't like that their choir director didn't always show—who knew? Dad got another car somehow and Mom started substitute teaching to supplement our income, and off we were each Sunday to another town down the shore called Ocean City.

Ocean City was a dry town where "shoobies" would come and fill the beaches each summer. Shoobies came in from places like Philadelphia and filled up the non-alcohol-polluted beaches. Their lunches, from what we were told, were packed in shoe boxes, hence the name "shoobies." We were not shoe box people because we were from a nearby oceanside town, where we lived even in the off season. I don't know how my parents found out about Ocean City Baptist Church, but we became members and Dad became the choir director once again. We were readily accepted into the folds of this church. We went to Sunday school every week, and we kids signed up for the Wednesday-night prayer groups and Bible studies that fit our age categories. Abi and Nate were in one together and I was in the younger group, which I hated. I, like any younger sibling, wanted to be accepted by the older kids and did everything in my power to make that happen.

After each group met in their separate rooms each Wednesday night, we would join in the church gym for basketball or some such recreation. This was my favorite part. I would sit on the sidelines, not too much of a sports chick myself, and stare at the older boys with eyes of lust and wonder. Why a nine-year-old recognized lusty eyes was an issue that would become obvious to me only later in my life. But then, I was just doing what I thought was natural to a girl. I would flirt heavily with whomever I thought was cute, and would do it in a way that was subtle enough to be considered good and Christian.

There was one boy I really liked. I think my sister did too, but I didn't care. His younger brother was in my group and had a crush on me, I could tell. But I wasn't interested in boys my own age. I liked them older and wiser. When we were Methodists, Nathan would bring home his nice Methodist friends sometimes and we would build tents in the living room, and I would let them fondle and kiss me because I thought that was a normal thing to do. So a boy Abigail's age meant nothing to me; I had had older.

I'll never forget this dark-haired beauty of a boy. He would take his shirt off when they played basketball, and I would practically melt. I could tell he would notice me, even if he thought it was a no-no, and sooner than all get out David—that was his name— and I were having silent naughty sideline conversations. He would purposefully fumble the ball in my direction and when it rolled toward me, he would wink at me and grab back the ball, showing off for me. It worked. Boy oh boy, did it ever work. I was in love.

David and I carried on our sideline flirtation for months. Then sidelines expanded into curbsides and curbsides into pew sides. We would find each other after Sunday school and follow each other through the church to see where the other was sitting just so we could look at each other during the sermon. I was beginning to like church. Before David, I would get so frustrated I could barely sit still. My legs would get crampy and my head filled with things I couldn't ask about when it was over, so I had learned to hate church. But those times were quickly changing. I was up on Sunday mornings before anyone else. I could hardly wait to get to Sunday school just so it would be over and I could find David waiting for me, all dapper and casual by the staircase that led to the balcony. In the balcony we would sit pews apart but in the other's line of sight, so that no one noticed our dangerous affair of the mind. Sometimes David would slip me a note during our ascent and I would read it during the sermon and then bat my eyelashes at him, showing my approval. I would take a prayer-request card out of the pew in front of me and scribble something terribly risqué like "I like you too, Davey! Love, Anne" on the lines where I was supposed to be writing my request and then give it to him after church. He was my request. He was all I prayed I could have.

These terrible and torrid games continued like this ad nauseam until one day—

"Anne! Anne Celeste! Get in here!"

I was in the guest room down the hall from my parents' room playing my favorite game of detective. I was always looking for clues. Clues about what, I didn't know back then, but I'm certain I do now. I was a very good detective and I would make up all sorts of colleagues whom I would work with on my very complicated detective missions. I would play all of them. Some of us were good detectives and some of us weren't, which made the game more fun. When my father summoned me on this particular afternoon, I was looking in the top of a dresser that had a square cubbyhole in it meant for hats. But that day, hats were *not* what I was looking for. The cubby was a place where many many clues were hidden about my mysterious mission, and I was probably dusting for fingerprints.

"Anne Celeste, do you hear me? Get in here this second!" I quickly put my imaginary finger-dusting equipment into my pockets and told my colleagues that I would return in a flash.

"What, Dad?" Mom was in the room too. She was holding a wooden spoon.

"Oh, hi, Mom. What's up?"

They both had especially stern expressions on their faces. "What's up? You're up. What's this, young lady?" Dad was holding up a crumpled piece of prayer request in his hand. "Is this what you see fit to be doing when you're supposed to be listening to the *Word of God?*"

Mom had found a note that David had written to me in one of my very private places in a drawer in my room. A very *private* place! I didn't know what to say. I was caught, prayer-handed.

"How long has this been going on?" How long? A long time, but I didn't want to say that.

"Not long," I said instead, thinking that the shorter the period of time, the less amount of wooden-spooning I would get.

"Do you have any idea how old this boy is? What are you doing passing love notes in church to a boy much older than you? You should know better than that, young lady. You're never to see him or talk to him again. Do you understand me? *Do you understand?*"

"Answer your father, Anne Celeste!" my mother scolded.

"I understand. I'm sorry. I'll never do it again." I was so sad, so afraid. What was I going to do? How was I going to tell David that our affair was no longer a secret and no longer in existence? I couldn't bear the thought of never talking to or seeing him again. He was my life. My *whole existence*!

I don't think I felt the spooning on that day; I was too upset. I was a good girl and I wanted to do everything that my mother and father told me to do, but this was just too much. I was in love. When I showed up at Wednesday-night Bible night, David was waiting for me. It wasn't just my parents who had found out—his parents had found out too! I was way too young for David. I was nine and he was twelve. His parents were as upset with him as mine with me. We cried and hugged each other by the side of the church. It was the first real contact we had had and it felt so good, better than we had imagined.

"I don't care what they say, Anne. I love you." He loved me? Oh, my God!

"I love you too, David," I heard myself saying.

"Nothing will keep us apart! Nothing!"

The next week in church David showed up with a very pretty blond-haired girl his own age and sat next to her in the balcony. I was confused and hurt but couldn't say anything because my parents were keeping a close eye on me. I did all that I could to make eye contact with Dave, but I got nothing. I sat in church alone that Sunday and filled out the prayer card in front of me for real this time.

Please pray for me that I will get my boyfriend back.

I didn't put my name on the card because I thought the preacher wouldn't pray for a nine-year-old jilted lover. If I kept it anonymous, he might think it was for someone much older and more deserving. I dropped my request in the collection plate as it passed and prayed that my prayer would be answered.

CHAPTER FOUR

HEAVEN ON THE SEVENTH

Mom called it "Heaven on the Seventh," like it was a title of a song or something that we should know but none of us did. It became clear that Dad was not paying any rent or mortgage or whatever he was supposed to be paying on our house in Ventnor, so we were moving again. "Heaven" was a condo building not far down the boardwalk from Ocean City Baptist. It was situated on the beach, so it was ritzy enough for Dad to call home. The first order on the agenda was planning Susan's wedding.

One night we all got called down the hallway to our parents' bedroom. When we arrived, they were just hanging up the phone and had tears in their eyes. Susan had just gotten engaged! Susan had an on-again, off-again boyfriend all through college whose name was Judson. He was tall and handsome and Christian and Swedish and

wanted to get a job that would pay him a lot of money once he grad-
uated. He was perfect! We all approved of Jud, Mom and Dad especially. Susan was going to marry someone who would be rich. Rich
and handsome—our family's two priorities. We couldn't wait to see
the ring. Susan was doing exactly what my parents wanted her to
do—follow in their footsteps.

We all pitched in with thoughts of what she should wear, who
should be invited, and what roles we would all play. I was to be the
flower girl, which I hated because it meant I was young. Abi was
going to be a bridesmaid and Nathan a groomsman, something that
made Jud a real sport. I don't know if Nathan wanted to be in the
wedding, but Dad wanted it—so it was going to happen if Jud
wanted Dad's approval. And who didn't want Dad's approval?
Jud's parents were quite conservative, according to Susan, so she
wanted to wear a dress that expressed her individuality and creativity. This is where Dad came into play. We set off to showrooms
and antique boutiques from the shores of the Atlantic to the ports of
PA to find Susan a dress that said all she wanted to say without scar-
ing anybody away.

Susan ended up in a dress with gold sequins from head to toe
that was described to her as a mermaid's gown. Worn, it was said,
"by a movie star in the thirties."

Well, that sold us all. Dad loved the movies, I wanted to be in the
movies, and Susan looked like a movie star. Surely she would
sparkle and glisten as she walked down the aisle, and the dress, not
being the virginal white, would cause enough of a near heart attack
in Jud's conservative Swedish parents to let them know who was in
charge.

Dad must have borrowed money from one of his lovers in New
York or convinced Jud's parents to pay for the wedding, because it
was gorgeous. White on white on white, the room was filled with
glorious flowers and food and cake and rice—everything that a
daughter would want. Susan looked so stunning in her gown you
could hardly find air in the room to breathe. Abi wore a creamy
bridesmaid dress that Susan had picked from a store in New York,

and I was wearing a lacy number that my mother's rich twin sister had pulled from her daughter's closet. Mom was in a complete mother-of-the-bride ensemble—and it was all so incredibly perfect. Everyone gasped when Susan walked down the aisle. She was such a vision in her glittery gown that as I stood in the front of the church I made a pact that I would wear her gown one day when I was married so I could be just like her.

It only took a phone call a day later to realize that Susan didn't have it all like I had imagined that she had. She ran away the night of her wedding, but apparently changed her mind because she's still married to this day. I wasn't told the details of the story, but I wondered what had happened to make her run. I wondered why no one questioned what she was feeling, and then I remembered that no one ever asked what anyone was feeling in our family. She had gotten married in front of God and preacher and friends and friends of friends, so I assumed there was no turning back.

Susan's wedding happened around Thanksgiving, and so the next event was Christmas. She had made up with Jud and the two of them were coming to the condo to celebrate with us. Jud had told Susan of a Swedish tradition called Santa Lucia in which girls put wreaths of candles on their heads and serve coffee cake on Christmas morning, so Abi and I donned wreaths of fire to welcome the guy Susan had run away from into our family.

The presents that year had a very specific intention. Abi and I opened gifts of gel-like rouge and mascara and frosty-blue eye shadow. Mom and Dad had gotten it in their heads that we children could be making a living for the family if we spruced up our looks a little bit. Dad's exposure in the big city to fame and beauty had convinced him that his children could also become commodities. He had heard of "cattle calls" for shows where children got discovered, and since we could sing, why not give it a shot? If Broadway musicals didn't call our name, surely we could have careers doing commercials.

Soon Abi and I didn't walk out of the house without full-on

rouged-up faces, and when we tried we would be gently reminded that we looked a little better with a set of lashes that could be seen. After all, we were blond and the hairs on our eyes were a bit hard to see. It didn't take long before we were standing in front of a photographer, posing with pigtails. We each got a card of three pictures showing us in three different forms of identity. My card had me jumping in the air with a huge smile on my face in one corner, sitting on a box looking sexy in another, and staring seriously ahead in a bodysuit in another. In all the photos I was fully made up. I was nine.

Before you knew it, Mom had us enrolled in jazz class and voice lessons, but that only lasted a couple of sessions because we couldn't afford any more than that. Once cast in a commercial or starring in a Broadway show, we would resume the classes with our own money.

I don't know when I realized that this whole dream of our father's was retarded. Maybe it was when I was standing in a line around the block at an *Annie* cattle call in New York City, or maybe it was after I didn't get a callback. But surely I felt retarded. I couldn't sing like a Broadway star. I could sing a hymn in church, where people loved it because they had no other options.

It was after they didn't call my name off the list of callbacks that my father put his arm around my shoulder and said that with a little more practice I might become something worth casting. *Become something worth casting?* Was that all he wanted? I dejectedly walked out of the theater feeling like a complete and utter loser. I was no Brooke, that was for sure, and I felt my father's disappointment. When we were walking down the street in silence I wondered how I was going to tell my mother that I didn't get asked to return the next day. How was I going to tell her that they didn't want me? We had saved a lot of money for my bus ticket and had such high hopes that I would play an orphan, any orphan! And that's when I felt a tap on my shoulder. "Excuse me."

I turned around, thinking that it was my father playing a trick, but it wasn't. It was a man in a black coat carrying a briefcase. "Yes? Can I help you?" I was always so polite.

"You look like the exact kind of girl that we're looking for to be on the show *To Tell the Truth*. Do you know that show?"

I didn't, but before I could say so, my father piped in, "Sure she does! What are you looking for?"

The man started describing this whole show they were doing for which they needed someone to impersonate a girl who had been a friend of Amy Carter's and got to spend the night at the White House. The man thought that I looked like the right age and wanted to know if I would be interested in taking a meeting to see if I could lie well enough to fool people into thinking that it was me who had spent the night.

"Of course she'll take the meeting. Does she get paid for that kind of thing?"

"If she's convincing enough that the people on the panel think it's her and not the real girl that visited, she will."

Well, that's all it took for my dad to say yes. The next day we were sitting in the waiting room at whatever network *To Tell the Truth* was on. I was called into a room where a man sitting behind a desk asked me all sorts of questions to find out how well I could lie. I started giggling uncontrollably. I thought it was a supersilly idea that I would pretend that I had been to the White House when I hadn't been.

"I don't know if I'm the right person for the job, Mister." I don't know what made me so direct, but it would become a habit. "But I have an entire family who can lie. Maybe you want them to do your show."

I pulled out a postcard of our family in a picture-perfect pose. My parents had the photographer who had taken our composite shots take a picture of the family and then turned it into postcards. I had one on me and pulled it out of my pocket.

"This is my family." I showed the picture to the man. "My dad is in the waiting room and the rest of us live in Ocean City, New Jersey, and if this job could possibly pay any of us any money it would be greatly appreciated."

I gave the man our phone number and my father got a part, my mother got a part, and my brother got a part, all pretending to be people they weren't. It was a job made in heaven. Kitty Carlisle and one or two other celebs on the panel voted for members of my family, so each made a couple hundred dollars and received a box of cleaning supplies from the sponsors. Who knew then that cleaning supplies would be the way of our future?

•   •   •

Gas and oil, ammonia and soil . . . similar, no? I don't know who came up with the idea, but soon our family had boxes of cleaning supplies everywhere, and I mean everywhere. The condo was piled high and ideas were on the fly. We were going to become rich by selling cleaning supplies supplied by this company called Amway. Amway's products were the "Absolute Best!" as described to us with big smiles by our mother and father. "They're all-natural and don't harm the environment!"

Since when did we care about the environment? I don't think I had ever heard the word before. What the heck is the environment?

"We're going to sell these products to make a lot of money to buy a house so that when my deal comes through next Tuesday, we'll have made some money in the interim. Isn't it a swell idea, kids? And you're going to help!" We were going to make money in a week? A deal is coming through next Tuesday? What? Who?

"If the deal is coming through next Tuesday, then why do we have to sell cleaning supplies? And, besides, we're only kids—what business do we have selling things that won't harm something we've never heard of?" we might have said, but most certainly didn't, because before we knew it we were sitting in front of a white board that looked like a chalkboard, was the size of a chalkboard, but was *not* a chalkboard.

"Look at this nifty Magic Marker board, kids. Isn't it neat? You can write on it with this"—Dad wrote with a marker handed to him by my mother—"and erase it like this!" Mom handed him an eraser that looked very much like a chalkboard eraser but was *not* a chalkboard eraser.

"Isn't that neat? Look, I'll do it again." He did it again. "Neat, right?"

"Superneat, Dad. What's it for?" Well, Mom was going to have to explain what it was for because Dad hadn't actually stayed in the room when it was described to the group of suckers that they were suckered into by some other people who had been suckered before them. Dad had had some gas and oil stuff to attend to apparently, while Mom had stayed and listened.

"You see, when you start you have this amount of detergent"— she was drawing a graph and pointing to a line depicting the detergent—"you are at the bottom level, like dirt." She grabbed for another color marker. "But as soon as you sell all of this detergent"—she circled the line—"you climb to *this* level!" She drew a line from the circle. This line was green. "This means that you are at the *emerald* level and you get a bonus of more money. After the *emerald* level you can get to the"—she grabbed for a red marker and drew a line and a circle—"*ruby* level and get another money bonus. And after the *ruby* level you get to the"—here came the blue marker—"*sapphire* level, where you get another money bonus that's an even bigger bonus than the *ruby* level bonus and after that—" She kept drawing and circling and graphing like a madwoman—"And then you get to the *diamond* level, where there is such a big money bonus that you can buy any car or house or yacht or *diamond*!—ha-ha—that you want!"

Squeak! Mom's octave also pitched when she was excited about something she didn't really know about.

Dad starting applauding and chimed to her squeak, "And guess who the entertainment is for the next Go Diamond Weekend?"

Squeak!

Oh, my God, no. This was not happening. Dad had signed us up to be the entertainment at the rally for this cockamamy charade. Mom had plans to make red taffeta dresses for the girls and red taffeta shirts for the men so we all looked like shiny window treatments. She had already bought the patterns.

"Isn't it exciting, kids? Can't you hear it already?"

Dad started humming and Mom started humming, and next thing you knew we were standing in front of thousands of people who were cheering, "Go Diamond! Go Diamond! Go Diamond!"

All this in time to my father's fist pumping in the air like a painted fan at a football game after a touchdown. It was only when he felt the audience at their peak of frenzy that he slid onto the piano bench and pounded out the intro that was our cue:

> *Go tell all your friends*
> *And join up today.*
> *We're going to be diamonds.*
> *Amway! Amway!*

CHAPTER FIVE

THE HOUSE THAT JACK BUILT

On Christ the solid rock I stand.
All other ground is sinking sand.
All other ground is sinking sand.

Mom and Dad should have listened to the wisdom of the lyrics they were singing each Sunday because next we were moving into a house built on the sand. The walls that held our secrets were getting thinner and thinner and less and less sturdy. Our house was on stilts. Stilts on the sand. Some guy, let's call him Jack, got it in his head that he could make a lot of money building cheaper-than-shit houses on the beach that basically balanced on four pilings jutting out of the sand. The ocean, being not quite far enough away, would crash under the house at high tide. Surely we were going out to sea, but did it have to be this literal?

For our celebration of the move, we dressed ourselves in black shirts and jeans and headed to the jetty outside of our house to do another family photo. We were a year older, after all, and thought it would be nice to update our vanity. We posed with our blond hair blowing in the ocean breeze and smiled like we were the Von Trapps on holiday. My mom thought it would be clever to put a saying at the bottom of each card as a special little something that would make our postcards stand out from the other family postcards. (How many family postcards have you seen?) The picture that was decided on after much deliberation was a full-body shot with all of us on a different rock looking out at the camera with salt-glow expressions that said: "Hire us!"

The caption underneath read, WE'LL SEE YOU ON THE OCEANS OF THE WORLD! What that meant, who knows? Maybe she thought that there were some people like Jonah who were going to be spit onto our shores. Your guess is as good as mine. So we wanted to meet some people on the ocean, but didn't want a house on it for long. Dad had bigger and loftier ideas for where we would live: "Once the deal comes through next Tuesday!"

The reason that the other deals hadn't come through on the other Tuesdays was because he was now working on an even bigger deal that made the other deals obsolete. This deal was going to be so very big that we were going to become millionaires instantly. Once millionaires, we would have to live like millionaires, so we needed to find a millionaire's house.

It was my twelfth birthday when we set off to go find our mansion. On one of Dad's business trips he had visited a place called Scarsdale, New York, which is one of, if not *the,* richest suburbs outside of Manhattan. We piled into the car excited as all get out at the possibility of living in a mansion the next week. We drove about three hours and arrived in truly the most mansion-filled place I'd ever seen. Dad had set it up with a Realtor to show us around for part of the afternoon until our scheduled meeting at a boarding school that was, according to Dad, "the most prestigious school in the world." And then he added, "We want you kids to have the *best* education that money can buy, don't we?"

Well, who were we to say we didn't? The only problem with Dad's plan was that Nathan was now a junior in high school and didn't want to move for his senior year and leave all of his friends. If we waited a year, Abi would be a senior and it wouldn't be fair for her either. I was going to be in the ninth grade, so it wasn't as big an issue for me.

"Kids change schools for high school all the time! And you're thrilled at the prospect of going to one of the most prestigious schools money can buy, aren't you?"

Well, who was I to say that I wasn't? I wanted to live in one of these houses that we were going to see. Each one the Realtor took us through seemed more impressive than the one before. We gooed and gaaed because who wouldn't goo and gaa? There were houses with tennis courts and horse stables!

"We can have horses too! Abi, you've always wanted to ride, haven't you? Well, now you'll be able to!" That was really exciting. Even though it was Abi that had wanted the horses, I now wanted horses too. "Can I have a horse?"

"Of course, of course! You'll see. I'm going to make up for everything that you've lacked, kids. Just wait until next Tuesday."

We couldn't wait. We traipsed through kitchens the size of our house and thought of the meals that we would cook in them. We picked out bedrooms that had tiled floors and their own bathrooms and watched ourselves bathing in them. We sat in living rooms and imagined parties filled with friends we didn't yet know gossiping in them. It was fun. Superfun. We could barely get enough of the fun.

"Which do you like best?"

We all drooled and debated.

"I like that one!"

"No, I like the one before with the rose garden."

"The rose garden? Since when are you a gardener?"

"Since when we move into that house!"

We laughed and played and ran through lawns of green until it was time for the appointment at the school. We politely told the Realtor how sorry we were and we would love to see more, but we had an appointment to enroll us all in the school down the road. She was impressed and said something about it being one of the most of the most and we nodded our agreement and said we would be in touch. We piled back into the car and started singing one of our all-time favorites.

God is so good. God is so good.
God is so good. He's so good to me.

We drove down a long drive and through huge arches to the dean's office at this prestigious place, and Mom and Dad sang praises about what good kids we were. We were then led into a room down the hall where we sat to take enrollment tests or IQ tests—who knew which—and prayed that we would be smart enough to get in. When we finished taking the tests the nice dean took us on a tour of the school and we had dinner in the cafeteria. Mom and Dad were sure we would get in, and from the looks on Abi's and Nathan's faces they were pretty ready to screw staying at Ocean City High.

On the way back we decided on a house. Everyone was allowed to have at least one of the things they really liked, so we put our likes in order of most important for us to be happy and said what we wanted most. Three hours later we had made our decision. The three-million-dollar home would be purchased the second the deal came through.

There's a place for us. A time and place for us.
Hold my hand and we're halfway there.
Hold my hand and I'll take you there.
Somehow . . . Someday . . . Somewhere . . .

Tuesday came and went and came and went and . . . came . . . and . . . went. Suddenly it was Christmas again. Abi made the decision to skip her junior year to graduate with Nathan so that she wouldn't have to move into the mansion when she was a senior.

>*We'll find a new way of living.*
>*We'll find a way of forgiving!*
>*Somewhere . . .*

• • •

Susan and Judson had moved to Virginia so Jud could go to business school there. They had a new apartment we all wanted to see, so off we went for Christmas Day. Abi and I bought stuff for wreaths of candles and that was to be our present to the family. By now each of the kids had gotten jobs doing what they could do to help out. I worked at a greasy hamburger stand on the boardwalk close to the house where I would sing *Annie* songs to attract the customers. So the audition wasn't all a loss. At the stand I would ask the nice people what they would like and if they wanted more music, then I would sing as I got them their fries or shake. Abi got a job waitressing; no restaurant served alcohol, so she didn't have to be twenty-one. It wouldn't have mattered anyway, because she looked twenty-one or near to it even though she was only fifteen. Nathan delivered papers, stacked papers, and stacked sandwiches at a local deli during the day, and worked at a boardwalk pizza joint at night. It was clear that this was not going to be a present-giving Christmas when Dad took all of our money that month to travel to New York.

Susan made wonderful coffee cake to serve for the fire presentation, and we all sat around talking about the house that we were going to move into in Scarsdale.

"I'm sorry it hasn't happened yet, kids, but it will. Until then, I got you this!" Dad was pulling something out of his pockets that I hoped weren't more pictures of Brooke. I was not disappointed. Dad handed us each a sheet of yellow legal paper that had been folded into three sections and had our name written in red on the outside. We were instructed to open our letters all at the same time, read what it said, and then read them out loud to the group one by one. We all looked at each other and looked at the papers and then opened them. I didn't see the expressions on the others' faces because I was so excited by what mine said.

"Dad promised me a trip to Russia! Oh, my God, I'm going to go to Russia!" I jumped up and hugged my dad as hard as I could. "Thank you, Daddy! Thank you! Thank you for my trip to Russia!"

Everyone laughed and cheered for my dream coming true and then proceeded to read the gifts out loud from their letters. We had all been promised the things that we most wanted. Nathan got flying lessons, Abi a horse, Susan and Jud a new house, and Mom a cruise around the world. We were beside ourselves. It was so sweet and so thoughtful and so in the spirit of Christmas that we didn't even mind it when he said, "And it's all going to happen after next Tuesday."

Susan put on a Lionel Richie album and Dad held out his hand for my mother to dance.

We celebrated our Christmas with tears in our eyes as we watched the two of them spin across the floor. It would be the last time we saw our parents embrace.

• • •

The phone got turned off, which should have been a sign. But we were always optimistic. There was a pay phone that we used as our house phone on the boardwalk, and we would leave the door open to see if we could hear it over the crashing waves. Sometimes we did, sometimes we didn't. Sometimes we had a hard time explaining why we couldn't shut the window to the people on the other end of the line when the noise of the waves was too loud for us to hear what they were saying, and we would have to ask them to yell.

One day after school it would sink in that we didn't have to worry about paying the phone bills anymore because there was no phone. No phone and no house either. I had about a three-block walk from the bus stop home, and when I got to the end of the block closest to the house I saw my family gathered on the steps leading up to the door. I figured we had been locked out. And I was right. So locked out we wouldn't be allowed in again. Jack had had the locks changed and the door boarded up with yellow tape and signs reading KEEP OUT! and NO ADMITTANCE! like our house was a crime scene.

And it was, really. Without much explanation from Dad, we were ushered into a borrowed Cadillac that was in the driveway just waiting to take us someplace we did not yet know. There was complete silence until we arrived at someone's door in Atlantic City. It was dark and I don't know if he woke this man up, but there was arguing and confusion and more arguing before Dad had a set of keys in his hand and was driving us someplace else.

Apparently, Dad had convinced the man he had been speaking to to give him the keys to a house that the man was selling. He was a Realtor whom Dad had known from his past or present and was his lover or not his lover—somehow he was connected to him enough to trust my father in a house that belonged to neither of them. We needed a place to stay for the night, to say the least, so we pulled up to this stranger's home, parked in the driveway, and loaded into the house. In hushed tones we were instructed to find bedrooms, as if the walls were going to hold the sound of our voices and tell the owners the next day that we had been there. We, this family of five, spent the night in a person's house whom we did not know and were most definitely never going to meet. We slept with our eyes open, wondering what in God's name was going to happen to us next.

CHAPTER SIX

THE MERRY MACS

"Welcome home!"

The Macs stood at the back door of their modest two-story house with arms open to us as we ascended the staircase leading up to their kitchen. We hugged them and they hugged us like we had been planning all along to move in with them and were thankful that the day had finally arrived after all the anticipation.

"Come in. Come in." They cleared the way for all five of us to get through the door and into the kitchen where their children were waiting.

"Hey! Welcome! Isn't this great?"

Scotty and Steven were the Macs' two sons. Steven was best friends with my brother and fooled around with Abi sometimes after

Bible study. Scotty was a freshman in college and one of the most handsome guys around town. Their daughter, Sandra, was living at home while attending nursing school. All of them were standing in the kitchen with bright eyes, making us feel as welcome in their home as anyone could. The Macs had had a family conference after Nathan told Steve that we were homeless and had agreed to take us in.

There is no way to describe my utter amazement about their generosity. We were a family of five and they were a family of five. She was a secretary and he a schoolteacher. They put food in our mouths, a roof over our heads, and clothing on our backs for more than a year and never once complained of the burden. Instead, they moved Sandra to the attic and Scotty in with Steven and gave our family two of their bedrooms to live in.

"This is where we eat breakfast. The cereal's in here." Mrs. Mac was opening cabinets filled with food such as we had never seen. "Help yourself to anything at any time. We love you and we're glad you're here."

Scotty threw his arms around me. "Yeah, really glad."

I don't know if we could even eke out a thank you. We were holding our bodies like statues, afraid that a sound escaping would break us apart and we would shatter onto their floor. What was happening was indescribable. We moved like one unit through their house as they gave us a tour.

"This is the dining room. We eat together at night unless one of the kids has a game. Then we're at the game." Scotty and Steven both played sports.

"This is our favorite room—"

"Yeah, this is where I'm going to beat you at backgammon, Annie," Scotty said and then messed my hair. They called me Annie, all of them—a term of endearment, a familiarity. It sounded so wonderful, playing a game. I didn't know what the game was but I couldn't wait to be beat. It was a family room and it showed. There were magazines and comfortable chairs. "And this is the living room. As you can see, we're not very formal in this house." The living room was a continuation of the family room. It looked lived in, relaxed. Homey. And they were welcoming us into it.

"I'm excited, I've always wanted to have sisters," Sandra said as we walked up the stairs to the room she was moving out of in order for Abi and me to move in. "It's not much, but . . ."

Not much? Not much? We were homeless. We had nothing. With each step it was sinking in more and more. Who did we think we were, kicking people out of their bedrooms so that we could have a place to sleep? I felt dirty. My skin was disappearing inside of itself. I wanted to be dead, dead or gone. I felt like a slug.

"Thank you, Sandy. Thank you so much."

Abi and I tried to blend ourselves into one person so that they wouldn't notice that we were there. One girl was less than two. Scotty flipped the switch of the light in his room and I saw my father look around with disdain. A teenage boy's room was not where a millionaire lays his head.

"And here's the boys' dorm." Steve had crammed three single beds into his room, one for Nathan, one for Scotty, and one for himself. "Cool, right?"

Supercool. Oh, God, was it cool. I scanned the room and saw a basketball hoop, a dartboard, a baseball bat . . . It was so normal. It was all so normal, except that it was the most disturbing reality any of us could imagine.

I don't know if they thought it would be a week or two before we got back on our feet, but after a month or two, we kids were getting pretty uncomfortable. I tried my best to disappear whenever I could, joining cheerleading squad, student council, church choir, bell choir—anything I possibly could to not be in the house and not be seen. I baby-sat at night and would encourage parents to take weekend breaks so that I could stay over someplace else and give the Macs a break from seeing my face. We had suffocated ourselves and now we were suffocating another family. It was dreadful. We were embarrassed. Horrified. But we carried on like it wasn't happening, as we had been taught to do our whole lives. We sang in church on Sundays and kept our secrets hidden in our smiles.

*　　　　*　　　　*

Are you tired of chasing pretty rainbows?
Are you tired of spinnin' 'round and 'round?
Wrap up all the shattered dreams of your life,
And at the feet of Jesus lay them down.

As I was walking out the door for choir practice one Sunday afternoon, I was called into the living room and told to sit down. Nathan, Abi, and my parents were seated already.

"I'm giving you an ultimatum, Don. Get a job this week or get out." There had been screaming and fighting in the house for weeks now. The Macs had sat with my parents behind closed doors and said things we children weren't allowed to hear but knew anyway. Dad's delusions about the gas and oil business were stronger now more than ever. He refused to face the reality that we were broke and he took no responsibility. My mother was at her wit's end, and so were we.

"I'll get a job, I promise, I'll get a job."

After Dad moved out I asked my mother why she wouldn't get a divorce. She was horrified at the suggestion. "I will not be a divorcée, Anne. I'll be a widow."

•　•　•

With Dad gone it was like we had done spring cleaning. We resolved to get out of the Macs' without Dad's help. He had put us in so much debt that we couldn't get a bank account, so Mom's top dresser drawer became the bank. Envelopes were marked on the flaps for each thing we needed to save for: tithe 10%, rent 70%, food 10%, gas and electricity 10%. We would divide our money with each paycheck. We had a goal and we were determined to do everything in our power to make it happen.

The first order of business was to double up on jobs. We all took another. The family that I had been baby-sitting for on the weekends owned a dinner theater and they were casting a rendition of *The Music Man.* They wouldn't promise anything, but if I wanted to audition for the director to play the role of Amaryllis, I would have an equal shot with everyone else. Well, Swainton, New Jersey, was hardly Broadway, but who cared? I learned the songs that I was supposed to sing in the show and belted them out for the director as best I could. When I got the part I nearly fainted. It wasn't so much that I was cast in a show, I was going to be making one hundred dollars a week. *One hundred dollars a week!* My contribution to the family funds was going to be tremendous. And boy oh boy, dinner theater! Blue-haired ladies and Shirley Temples to my heart's content!

Although I was the youngest member of the troupe, I was embraced as one of the family. I was comfortable here with these struggling actors on their way to becoming stars. I made friends and had my eyes opened to the world of theater and fun and people doing what they wanted to be doing. There was joy here, and I determined that joy was where I wanted to live.

Mom had been working as a secretary at a brokerage firm called Prudential-Bache. We liked the name because it rhymed with our last name. Mom would say it with pride when she picked up the phone: "Hello, this is Nancy Heche at Prudential-Bache." I don't think it was just her cheery rhyme that made her boss think she was too smart for the job. She was simply too smart. This housewife of twenty-five years was going to become a stockbroker and her boss was going to pay for her training. We were flabbergasted. Our mom a stockbroker? This was just too much!

"Anne Heche, please report to the principal's office immediately. Anne Heche to the principal's office."

I was being called to the principal's office? I never did anything wrong. All the kids booed and hissed as I scooted out of class toward the ominous doors at the end of the hallway.

"What's wrong?" I asked the secretary who was waiting.

"You have a phone call. You can take it in that office over there." I closed the door behind me. "Hello?"

"Guess what?" I heard my mother saying with a tone of voice that sounded hopeful, which was nice for a change.

"What?" The suspense was killing me. "What?"

"We got our first credit card, Anne. Our first credit card!"

"Oh, my God! You're kidding!" I started jumping up and down. I'm sure I looked like my composite shot picture to the secretary who was staring at me through the glass.

"I just called Nate and Abi and wanted you to know too. We did it, honey. We did it!"

With plastic in our purses we were finally able to get a lease of our own, but all of our furniture was behind locked doors. Mom convinced Jack that it was Dad's fault that we hadn't paid rent on the beach and pleaded with him to *please* show us some mercy. After some sweet talking, some good old-fashioned begging, and a reclaimed painting Mom and Dad had given Susan for a wedding gift, Jack handed over a sofa, the washer/dryer, and our beds.

Soon we were loading the pink-and-black sectional Dad had picked for the beachhouse look into an apartment on the top floor of a Realtor's office called Haagar. The apartment was tiny, but had three rooms. There was a little breakfast nook that doubled as a dining room and had a lovely view of the alley. We were so proud of ourselves we could spit. We were actually paying our rent for the first time in our lives. We had earned our money the old-fashioned way—we worked for it.

CHAPTER SEVEN

HOME AT HAAGAR

Dad had moved to New York City after getting kicked out of the Macs' but he never got a job. Once in a while Abi and I took trips to New York to visit and give him some money, but things were awkward. He was still promising diamonds and houses, but we no longer believed him. We knew he was delusional. His mind and body were deteriorating more and more each time we saw him, but he would never admit that he was sick. The most he would say was that he had hepatitis again. We knew that was a lie, but we didn't know what was wrong. Sometimes we would be walking arm in arm and he would collapse on the curb, unable to get a breath. He would promise me that nothing was wrong and then he'd disappear for hours at a time.

"I'll meet you back at this corner in a few hours, okay? This exact corner." Before I could answer he would be in a cab screeching away from me. I was thirteen years old, he was forty-five.

He would meet me back at the corner with his energy renewed, pretending nothing had ever happened, and we'd return to his apartment on the Lower East Side. "My roommate's out of town again," he would say every time. But I wasn't so stupid. Working in dinner theater had opened my eyes to a lot. I hope I don't blow any covers here, but dinner theater is teeming with gay men. Through my friendships with them I had come to terms with my father's hidden sexuality.

One night I decided to confront him about it, so I asked him where his "roommate" slept. He lied as usual and told me there was a bedroom up the steps before changing the subject. There was never a question where I would sleep. We always had the same routine. He would undress in front of me, climb naked into his bed, and hold out his hand for me to join him. That night, I resolved that I would never visit him again.

Dad died on March 4, 1983. His was one of the first cases of AIDS diagnosed in the United States. Dad never admitted that he was gay or that he was dying. When my mother visited him in the hospital with Abi and Nathan, he was so sick that he couldn't remember his family. I didn't go. Mom showed him a picture of me to jog his memory. But, no such jog. It was unclear back then how the disease was transmitted, and the doctors warned them that it would take about eight years before any of us would know for sure that we were clean. My mother knew nothing of the extent to which my father had touched me, but that didn't matter. AIDS was in a handshake or a kiss, the doctors warned. The fear of AIDS was so complete that no one in our town would recognize our father's death. We had to hold the memorial service at the Lambs Theatre in New York City where my father had been going to church because the Baptists in Ocean City wanted nothing to do with him. We listened to friends of my father's talk about a man we had never known. He had been leading a double life since before I was born. His shame of himself oozed into his family and left us with blood we would try to get out for the rest of our lives.

Three months to the day after my father's death, Nathan drove our car off a road and was killed.

• • •

"I would kiss you right now if your brother didn't just die."

It was Dave. Dave, the guy that I had been flirting with for five years behind my parents' back, was speaking in a sexy yet sympathetic enough tone into my ear. I was standing outside in the alley because the apartment was spilling over with people eating cold cuts. I guess the town figured they had to make up for never calling about my father so everyone was there for my brother. It was okay to mourn for an eighteen-year-old boy, just not his gross dad. It was all so pathetic. I wanted Dave to kiss me. I wanted anything to get me out of the space I was in, but I couldn't do it. Nathan was dead. My brother was dead.

I finished out my work at the dinner theater for a couple of weeks while my mother and I made arrangements to get out of town. Abi was going to attend Wheaton College in Illinois as planned and Sue and Jud were now in Chicago for his work. It seemed a logical place for us to go, if there was any logic to be found. My last night at the show we all cried for my parting. The owner of the dinner theater, who had become my very close friend, was going to drive me home for the last time. As I walked to the car in the pouring rain, I heard someone calling my name.

"Annie! Annie, wait!"

I turned around, and it really was like a scene in a movie. Rain mixed with tears was pouring down my face. The guy who was the lead in all the shows—the gorgeous hunky guy—was running after me. I got the chills and not because I was cold.

"Wait. I have something to tell you," he panted. I was going to die. Sal or Vito, or whatever his name was (he had two and I could never figure which was his stage name), had something to say to me?

I panted back, "What, Sal/Vito, what?"

He licked the raindrops from his lips. I wished I was a raindrop.

"I'm in love with you." He blurted it out like if he didn't say it at that moment, he was never going to say it. And he shouldn't have said it. "I haven't been able to say it until now because I know it's not right, but I love you. I've always loved you."

Glee would be the least of the awesome feelings that rushed through my body at that moment. You don't understand: Here was a guy whom I had been working with for two years, a guy I stood by at the host stand every night to help seat people just so I could be near him and smell him, a guy that *all* the girls drooled over backstage when he sang or simply walked by. This guy was *the* guy, and he was in love with me? No, no, no. *I* was in love with *him*.

We kissed a kiss of utter abandon and then kissed some more. He handed me a card with his phone number on it and told me to call him when I got to Chicago. We kissed and grabbed and kissed and grabbed until we were drenched from head to toe and I had to go.

I was fourteen years old. He was thirty-one.

• • •

A child of abuse knows no boundaries. A child of abuse wants to find love with whomever they can. A child of abuse thinks that love is bonded to sex. A child of abuse wants to make what their perpetrator has done to them okay so they re-create the action with other people. A child of abuse communicates sexually to show love. A child of abuse thinks that communicating sexually is the only way to receive love. A child of abuse thinks that if they do not show love through sexuality, there is something wrong with them. A child of abuse thinks that sex is wrong. A child of abuse spends their life trying to make sex right. A child of abuse has no healthy attachment to sex because it has been raped from them. A child of abuse recognizes a disturbed sense of sexuality as a place of comfort. A child of abuse can only function in abuse until they recognize the pattern and change it. A child of abuse has the near impossible task of making their sexuality their own and not their abusers'. A child of abuse lives in the shit and the shame of their abusers because it was put into their body each time they were touched by them. A child of abuse is not their abuse. A child of abuse thinks that they are.

• • •

"Mom . . . Mom? Are you there?"

"I don't know what else to say, Anne. Clearly you want me to say something, but I don't know what it is and it's getting late."

"Late? It's getting late? I've had to deal with this shit my whole life and it's getting late for you?"

"What do you want me to say?"

"A lot of things, Mom. I want you to say a lot. Like you're sorry. How 'bout that, Mom? How 'bout saying that you're sorry that your creepy fucking husband did this to me? How 'bout saying that you wish it never happened and you wish you could have done something to stop it? How 'bout saying that you should have taken me to the doctor so that you would have known and left that motherfucking asshole? How 'bout taking some fucking responsibility for what happened to your daughter while you were rocking yourself to oblivion singing songs about Jesus? *What about me, Mom? What about your daughter? Do you have* any *remorse about this? Do you feel bad, sad, angry, frustrated, mad . . . ?* ANYTHING? DO YOU FEEL ANYTHING ABOUT WHAT I'VE JUST TOLD YOU?"

I was up on my feet, pacing holes into the kitchen floor. I was sweating and licking the drops from my lips and spitting them into the phone. I couldn't believe how filled with rage I had become. I had promised not to get angry, but I never expected this. I never expected nothing.

"You've done a lot of work on yourself, Anne. I know it was hard to go through. I can hear it in your voice."

"YOU CAN HEAR IT IN MY VOICE? I BET YOU CAN! I'M SCREAMING AT THE TOP OF MY LUNGS TO GET SOME SORT OF RESPONSE FROM YOU, MOTHER. I BET YOU CAN HEAR IT! ARE YOU GOING TO DO ANYTHING ABOUT IT? ARE YOU GOING TO ACT LIKE MY

MOTHER FOR ONCE IN YOUR GODDAMN LIFE? CAN
YOU BE A MOTHER FOR ONCE?"

I was reaching, grabbing, gasping for a sign that this woman
loved me, that she heard me, that she was going to take care of me.

"I admire you for going through all of this. I wouldn't have the
courage to do what you've done."

I couldn't believe my ears. She was telling me that she was
choosing to live in denial because the truth was too painful. She
couldn't hear what I was saying because it meant that she would
have to open her own can of shit and shame and look at it. She
didn't want to look. She wouldn't look. She was choosing not to
look and she was admitting her weakness. She didn't leave my
father because she didn't know how. She didn't have the strength
to see him or question him because then it meant that she would
have to see and question herself, her decisions, her life. So she hid.
She justified her actions by saying that she was a good Christian
and good Christians didn't question their husbands. Good Christians didn't question their lives. Her religion had become her
shield, and she hid behind it with all of who she was. *My hope is
built on nothing less than Jesus Christ and righteousness.* She had
made her choice. Without it she was nothing. To see me she would
have to put her shield down and look at her life, look at her shield,
look at what had blinded her all these years, and there was no way
she was going to do that.

"Jesus loves you, Anne."

And she hung up the phone.

• • •

> *Jesus loves me, this I know,*
> *For the Bible tells me so.*
> *Little ones to him belong.*
> *They are weak, but he is strong.*
> *Yes, Jesus loves me. Yes, Jesus loves me.*
> *Yes, Jesus loves me. The Bible tells me so.*

It's curious to me that religion teaches that children are weak and Jesus is strong. Here we're taught this story of this guy Jesus who was born in a manger by this chick who had never had sex. Miraculously, Mary got impregnated by God and Jesus is God's son. Jesus grows up and tells everybody that he's God in the flesh and to follow him. So Jesus gets some followers, tells some more people that he's God, works some miracles, and a few years later gets hung on the cross. What's strong about that? I ask. *What's so strong about Jesus?* He's thirty-three and he's dead. This is the guy we're taught to put all of our faith in and he's dead by the ripe old age of thirty-three. If I had been allowed to ask questions, I surely would have asked why he couldn't save himself for living a bit longer. I mean, I don't know if I want to "belong" to that guy like the song says. Yeah, he got to go to heaven, but who's ever seen heaven and aren't we supposed to like it here on earth? Didn't God create it for that very purpose? Jesus *died* to show his love for me? Is that what my father did? Do we all have to die to show love? I'm confused.

CHAPTER EIGHT

THE BELDEN STRATFORD

"Help! Help! Help! The sky is falling! The sky is falling!"

It was appropriate that the first play I did in high school was an absurdist drama called *The Skin of Our Teeth,* written by Thornton Wilder. I was cast to play the lead role of Sabina, and I cried out those opening lines with more truth than anyone could know. The sky may well have fallen down. Mom and I were living in a residential hotel in Chicago called the Belden Stratford that was down the street from my school. We had a one-bedroom apartment and lived like we were roommates. Our beds touched side by side, so to get any privacy at all I had to sit in the closet. Sal/Vito and I would carry on an affair for more than a year as I sat on the floor huddled between my jeans and my underwear whispering sweet nothings over the phone to a man more than twice my age. At Thanksgiving I told my mother I was going to visit friends back in Jersey and stayed instead with him. We fooled around but didn't have sex. It was only after he tried to go further with me in the front seat of his car when he was dropping me off at the airport that I decided I needed to break it off.

Mom's affair was no better. She had started carrying on with a Jewish man before Dad died. In between sobs every night she would ask God to forgive her for the sin of falling in love with a married Jewish man. What she didn't know was that every time he called and spoke to me, he would tell me that he was in love with me, and couldn't we find some time alone next time he came to visit my mother? She really knew how to pick 'em. She broke off the affair after we went to her twin sister's house for Christmas and she was caught on the phone talking to—a married Jew! "In my house? Get out and take your children with you!"

My aunt was a loving Christian woman. After Abi, Mom, and I were pushed out the door of her house on Christmas Day, it was only appropriate that my mom would say, "This is how God punishes us for sinning. I knew I shouldn't have dated that married Jew." She was big on sinning, apparently, because next thing you knew she was seeing another Jew. The good thing about religion is that you can always pray for forgiveness, and pray . . . and pray. God doesn't say how many times he'll forgive you and, in my mother's case, she trusted an endless supply.

My continuing sexual excursions were no less sinful. I was in the terrible habit by now of denying everything that had happened to our family. I skipped school one day and found myself in the front seat of a car acting out some fantasy of a photographer I met. I was a hitchhiker who got in the car and gave him a hand job—no questions asked. He convinced me that it was an art project he was working on and held his camera to his eye as I jerked him off. When the art was complete, he dropped me off at the Häagen-Dazs where I worked after school. Besides fooling around with the various classmates I had crushes on, I was underage and having sex with a Chicago Bears player who picked me up at a bus stop in his very sporty big-dick car after he pulled over and said, "It's not fair, you standing out in the cold like that. Why don't you let me drive you?"

Abi wasn't lagging in the sexually fucked-up department either. She was kicked out of her Christian surroundings for having sex on campus (a Christian no-no) and was sent home to room with Mom and me. Three women in a one-bedroom apartment was, to say the least, cozy. Abi started doing drugs and eventually became a stripper. She said that she was hostessing at a restaurant downtown. When she showed up one night in a fur coat, she politely explained, "My customers like me, Mom."

Well, that's all the explanation my mother needed. The no-questions policy had turned into a few-questions policy and was replaced with an unspoken rule that if the truth was nowhere in the response, not to worry about it because the truth was too uncomfortable to know.

"The sky is falling! The sky is falling!"

My performance was received with great approval. So great, in fact, that one night after the show I was approached by a handsome woman carrying a hat.

"Ms. Heche?"

That was sweet.

"You can call me Anne."

"Anne, then. I really liked your performance tonight."

"Thank you. Thanks a lot." I wish I could remember her name, but it escapes me now . . .

"Have you always wanted to be an actress?"

"Oh, I don't know. I can't say I've decided I want to be anything except not dead." It was the truth.

"Well, would you maybe like to think about it a little more seriously and come to New York with me to audition for a soap opera?" A soap opera? I had no idea what a soap was, but—

"Would I ever! Are you serious?" She was serious. Soon Mom and I were jetting off to the big city and getting a tour of the set of *As the World Turns*. If only my father could have seen me then, he would have shit. They asked me to read a couple scenes with a boy on the show, and I guess it went well because I was called into the executive's office and offered the job. My mother said, "We'll have to think about it."

I wanted to cry. What was there to think about it? This was my way out—my future! My escape from the dorm! But Mom didn't want me to escape. Her son had died two years earlier and she was not about to let another child go. She was beginning to get on her feet as a broker, and moving to New York would be uprooting her when she was just beginning to feel settled again. I agreed that I didn't want my mother moving with me, even if I would be making more money than we had ever seen. I wanted to go without her, but that was simply out of the question. I turned down the job, thinking that my only chance to escape my mother's grasp had flown out the window.

• • •

My mother once told me that her only purpose for being here on earth was to get into heaven. When I asked her why she didn't just kill herself then, she told me it was because killing yourself is a sin and living here on earth was about suffering so that you would not suffer once you got to heaven. This strange logic carried me through my high school years. I often wondered why she didn't say that one of her purposes was to love her children, or herself. But she never did. She was here to love Jesus, she explained, so that she could get into heaven and be with God. When I asked her what heaven was, she matter-of-factly described a place where there were streets of gold and gates of pearls. It sounded a bit gaudy to me.

"And you're *sure* that this is what heaven looks like?"

"I'm sure."

"And how are you sure?"

"The Bible says so."

"And how are we going to get to heaven?"

"By accepting the Lord as your—"

"I know that part. But the world is going to end soon, right?"

"The Bible says so in Revelations, yes."

"And it will end because Jesus is going to come back, right?"

"Right."

"And how are we going to know that he's here?"

"The heavens will open up and he'll take all the believers with him."

"So if you're not dead yet when Jesus comes back, you'll see the heavens open up."

"That's correct."

"And if you're not a believer, what happens to you then?"

"You'll be sent to hell."

"So there's a place that's called hell and there's a place that's called heaven and they are both concrete, tangible places. Heaven is built with gold and pearls and hell is built with flames and they are both *real,* they are *not* metaphors for our state of mind. Is that what you're telling me?"

"That's what the Bible says, yes."

"God lives in heaven and the devil lives in hell, and they too are *real.*"

"God is a trinity of God, the Son, and the Holy Spirit, and I believe that they are in heaven, yes."

"And you believe that there is a devil?"

"Yes."

"So, hypothetically, if I don't believe what you believe, you believe that I will go to hell?"

"Yes."

"So when Jesus comes back, the heavens will open, and if I'm still alive, which is a definite possibility, I will be sent to hell with everyone who does not believe what you believe because what you believe is the only truth."

"It's the truth of the Bible, and I believe in the Bible."

"So you dedicate your life to loving Jesus because when he comes you want to ascend into heaven with him."

"If I'm not already in heaven when he comes back."

"Are you going to have a house in heaven?"

"I don't know the details of how I'll be living in heaven, Anne. I only know what the Bible tells me."

I don't think my mother ever expected that Jesus was going to come back in Fresno, California. But like she said, there are just some things the Good Book doesn't tell you.

• • •

Knowing that my mother's only purpose was to love Jesus made me understand that unless I was Jesus, I wouldn't receive her love. My fear was confirmed when she hung up the phone on me. So my dad loved movie stars and my mother loved Jesus. Dead people could love me, this I knew from the song, so I still had hope of getting what I wanted from my father. Jesus or movie star? Jesus or movie star? After careful and unconscious debate, I tackled the easier challenge first.

PART TWO

•

SURVIVAL
OF THE WEAKEST

CHAPTER NINE

ANOTHER WORLD

I had a hard time in high school, what with all the confusion about who I was and whether or not I was going to live or die. It was a hard subject to broach with potential friends.

"Hi, I'm Anne. I may be dying of AIDS because my father touched me. He's dead and so is my brother, but I'm completely well-adjusted. Do you want to be my friend?"

It was hard enough explaining why my mother and I lived in the same bedroom. Most teenagers are allowed at least some privacy. Most parents understand that the teen years are the time when kids begin to figure out who they are, explore themselves a bit. Talk on the phone, do homework, and learn how to masturbate. But not my parent. Not this teen. So my years in high school were a bit of a blur. All I wanted was out. I didn't know how I was going to make that happen, but happen it would. I think sometimes that if you wish hard enough, and your wish is in line with what's truly best for you, your wish will come true.

I got a call one afternoon while getting dressed for my hostessing job. It was the last in a series of every shit job a girl could have. I had moved up to restaurant work once I was a senior because I could lie better about my age, and although I didn't believe in wearing fur, I thought I might get some good tips.

"Is Anne there, please?"

"This is she." My mother had taught me proper English so I always knew the correct use of "her" and "she."

"You don't know me. My name is John Whitsell. I'm the executive producer on a show called *Another World.* You ever hear of it?"

I hadn't. "I'm sorry . . ."

"Don't worry about it. I'm not calling to give you a quiz. It's a soap opera that shoots here in Brooklyn, New York."

"Oh, a soap. I auditioned for one of those when I was a sophomore."

"That's right. I saw the tape of your audition and was wondering if you wanted to give acting another shot."

"You're kidding me."

John explained that the lady with the hat who had come to see me was a Procter & Gamble talent scout, and *Another World* was a P&G show as was *As the World Turns.*

"When there's a budding talent on the horizon, word tends to get out. I know you couldn't move in the middle of school, but you're a senior now and I thought it might be easier to make the break. There's a part on my show I think you may be perfect for. You interested?"

Was I interested? My faith was restored in God was how interested I was. My new savior was on the phone.

I flew to New York the night of a dress rehearsal for *Guys and Dolls,* and was scolded appropriately by the acting teacher in school.

"Soaps are shit, Anne. If you want to be a real actress, you'll have to learn better judgment and commitment. It's your dress rehearsal, for crying out loud! What do you think this says to the rest of the cast?"

I didn't care what it said, quite frankly. This was my ticket out, and I was going to take it. I showed up on a studio stage in NYC dressed in jeans and a Bahama Mama T-shirt. John met me at the door and instructed me to "pay no attention to the girls over there."

When I looked over, I saw the most incredible-looking women I had ever seen, all dressed in tit-popping numbers that I couldn't have fit my thigh into. I had accumulated some baby fat over the years and was what some might call a bit pudgy—my mother included. My mother had no restraint when it came to sizing me up about weight and how much of it I had.

"Turn around, Anne." She would make me stand naked next to Abigail to see who was chubbier. "Abi is looking quite fit today. I guess those aerobics classes are really paying off for her. Are you running after school as much as you used to?" I used to run around the lake come hell or high water and, according to my mother, I was slacking. "Maybe you should take some of the classes that Abi is taking."

She didn't know that Abi was stuffing her fingers down her throat after each meal. She didn't know that Abi tried to stick her fingers down my throat so that she would have company on her binge-and-purge missions. She didn't know that her constant criticisms would send one daughter into a bulimia treatment center after fifteen years, another into her own struggle with self-image, and the third into a spiral of self-hatred she only wished she could've puked her way out of, had she been able to hack the routine. She didn't know the secrets her daughters' bodies told. She didn't know that *my* body was beautiful and hanging on to pounds of shame and layers of mistrust.

"You could be an underwear model if you just lost some pounds around your hips, Anne. Put on that pair of Abi's underwear that makes her bottom look so good."

She would make us stand in our bikinis and watch us walk

across the room or the beach or wherever we happened to be to see who jiggled more, who could lose more, who could eat less.

"Could I be an underwear model, Mommy? Could I? Could I stand in front of a camera with no clothes on and show off my sexualized body to people that I don't know? Would that please you, Mommy? Would that mean I was beautiful, Mommy? If other people sexualize me, does that mean I'm beautiful? Did you see Daddy sexualize me, Mommy? Did you think that was beautiful? Could I please get more criticism, Mommy? I don't feel bad enough about myself. Could I have some more?"

When I looked at the girls whom John told me to ignore, I couldn't help but think that I should have exercised more, eaten less, listened to my mother.

"Bahama Mama, huh?" He was reading my shirt.

"We went there for Christmas last year."

"You like it?"

"Not really. I'm not much of a sun bunny."

"Oh? Why's that?"

"I can't stand wearing bathing suits."

I acted my ass off. At least that's what I heard after I returned home from the audition. They wanted me to come back for another screen test and bring an outfit that flattered my body a bit more. I rushed off to the Ann Taylor where I used to stock clothes and bought a low-cut number with my store discount.

"Glad you could make it back on such short notice." It was three days after the last audition.

"Are you kidding? I'm thrilled to be here."

"We're thrilled to have you." John was so nice to me. "This character's a little different than the last one."

"Yeah, I noticed."

"Not so much of a sexpot."

"Right." I couldn't help but think that I wasn't sexy enough to play the other girl. "I just want to see your range, that's all. Nothing to worry about. You did great last time, I just think this character might suit you a little better." I didn't believe him.

"Oh, okay."

He put his arm around me and took me to the stage where an actor was waiting to read lines with me. There were cameras and lights and—"Hey, nice outfit, by the way."

I was relieved. He didn't think my beige on beige on beige was too beige. He introduced me to the hunky guy standing in front of me. He was supercute, and I was glad about that because at the end of the scene I had to kiss him. I didn't know what that meant. Did they really kiss? Like kiss-kiss? Or did they fake it? When the actor stuck his tongue in my mouth at the end of the scene I got my answer.

"Cut!" I heard John yell out. "This is only rehearsal, guys. You can save the kiss for when we're rolling." The hunky guy turned pink.

"Anne, that was perfect. Now just relax into it. You want to put one on tape?"

"You bet your butt I do." I was shaking in my boots but had never felt more alive in my life. We did a few takes, kissed a few more times, and the dream was over.

John gave me a huge hug after the audition and said he would be in touch. It was three weeks before graduation and if he didn't call, I would have to go to college, and I didn't want to do that. I had had enough dorm life. I wanted to start living. I prayed every day that I would get the job. I prayed that God would forgive all the bad things I had done and love me enough to give me the part. You see, back then I thought God was a punishing God. He gave you things that you wanted when you were good, and made bad things happen to you when you were bad. A lot of bad had happened, so I figured that I was bad. Really bad.

"Anne?"

"Yeah?"

"It's John. John Whitsell. You remember me?"

"Of course I do, John. Of course I do." My heart was no longer in my chest. It was out the window, on a cloud where I prayed God would find it and hold it gently in his hands.

"How'd you like to come to New York after you graduate and join the cast of *Another World*?"

My heart flew back in the window and nestled itself back into my chest. I had been forgiven and God was telling me that I was good.

"Anne? You there?"

"*Yes!* Oh, my God, John. I'm here! Are you offering me the part? Did I get the part?"

"You got the part, Anne. You got the part!"

I started jumping up and down and screaming and laughing. I was getting out of the cage and I couldn't contain my glee. "I got the part! I got the part!"

John toasted me with his words: "Watch out, *Another World*— here comes Annie!"

A song welled in my throat and I just couldn't stop it.

> *I'm gonna be a part of it—*
> *New York, New York!*

I was kicking my legs like a proper Rockette and belting out the words like a hired Broadway babe.

> *If I can* (snap snap) *make it there,*
> *I'd make it* (snap snap) *anywhere.*
> *It's up to you* (snap) *New* (snap) *York* (snap)
> *NEW* (snap) *YORRRRRRKK!*

• • •

I dropped my bags in the sublet I had rented at One University Square and got into the black sedan that was waiting outside my door to take me to the studio in Brooklyn. There had been tears of rage and protest from my mother over my acceptance of the offer, but I told her that I was going to make the break with or without her support. I was now seventeen. It was the day after my graduation. The receptionist pointed me in the direction of John's office after welcoming me to the show, and I walked down the hall that would be my home for the next four years. John threw his arms around me and explained that the reason that I had done two auditions was because he wanted to see if I had enough range to play twins.

"Vicky and Marley. Vicky's the bad one, Marley's the good one. You'll play Vicky for the first few months until you get comfortable, and then we'll bring on Marley. The studio wanted someone else, but I fought for you. I believe in you, Anne. I know you won't let me down."

"Twins? I'm playing twins?"

"Yeah, twins. You think you can handle it?"

I didn't think I could, but I wasn't about to tell him that. "I think I can, if you think I can."

"I think you can."

"Then I can."

"Good. But don't worry about that now. All you have to worry about is today's scenes. You got the sides, right?" "Sides" is the term for scene pages in soap language—and movie language, but I didn't know that yet.

"Yeah, I got 'em."

"You memorize 'em?"

"Yeah, they're memorized."

"You like 'em?"

"Yeah, I like 'em."

"Good, 'cause I wrote 'em."

"I like 'em a lot."

"That's good. You should. I wrote 'em for you. Now go get dressed—or undressed, as the scene would have it. The wardrobe room is down the hall, around the corner, and on your right." I guessed it was time for me to leave his office.

"And, Annie?" I turned from the door. "I didn't do you any favors when I hired you. I want you here because I think you're the only one that can play these roles."

I didn't know what I had done to deserve such confidence, but I wasn't about to prove this man wrong.

As the story went, one of my characters, Vicky Love, had lost all her money at a casino in Vegas. She was sitting in a bubble bath in a fancier-than-shit suite and they had taken all her clothes so she couldn't leave the hotel without paying her debt. Her father was a millionaire (a for-real millionaire, not a fake one like my father) and she was calling him on the phone to come and bail her out. After much begging and pleading he would agree, but only if she came back to Hudson Valley or wherever the show took place, until she paid him back.

The costuming team poured me into a nude spandex number, unwrapped me from my towel, and dropped me in a steaming bubble bath to meet all the crew. I could not have felt more awkward. The nude spandex thing was a size fit for soap-sized girls, so my boobs were falling out and my ass was never in. I was grateful that John had paid attention when I told him that I hated wearing bathing suits.

"Everybody, this is Annie Heschee." A person with a walkie-talkie on his belt and a strange thing in his ear pronounced it wrong, of course, but I didn't bother correcting him. "She's the new Vicky/Marley."

After hellos all around we were ready for a rehearsal. I picked up the fake old-fashioned phone that was balancing on the edge of the tub.

"I talk into here?" I asked to anybody listening.

"Just like with a real phone," the director said.

"Right. But am I going to hear—" Before I could get out the question, I heard a man coming through the phone cord that was now dragging in the tub with my bubbles: "Can you hear me?"

"Hello?"

"Hi, I'm Kale. I play your father on this crazy show. I thought it was better to wait and meet you until you had some clothes on."

"Thanks," I stammered. What a nice guy, I thought.

"Congratulations. I've heard great things about you."

"Really?"

The person with a walkie-talkie was pointing at me. "Are we ready for a rehearsal?" I was as ready as I could be, falling out all over and practically peeing in the tub.

"Just relax," I heard Kale saying. "You're gonna be great."

Well, that was all the vote of confidence I needed.

"Ready!"

We rehearsed a little and I sucked a lot and we rehearsed some more and I sucked some more, and we carried on like that until I was ready to shoot and the bathwater had turned cold. Everyone was patient with me, and Kale tried to put me at ease by cracking jokes each time I made a fool of myself. When the day was finally over everyone applauded for me whether they meant it or not, but it wasn't about the acting, I realized. It was about support and it made me feel good and welcome.

"I think I'm gonna like having you as my fake daughter." I was dripping out of my robe, relieved that the day was over and I hadn't been fired.

"Kale?"

"Your one and only fake daddy." He was smiling. I was smiling.

"You must have had a really fucked-up childhood, kid." Wow. What an opener. I thought I hid it so well . . .

"It's that obvious? How could you tell?"

"Because we get along so great." He had been making jokes, but that wasn't a joke. He held out his arms and I fell in.

"I think I'm gonna like having you as my fake daddy."

"Well, then it's mutual liking. It's always better that way." He patted my wet head and some of my goose pimples fell onto his shirt. "Welcome home, kid. Welcome home."

• • •

Kale and I became fast friends. We talked about being fucked-up and the whys and the wheres and the whens of it all. I told him the little bits of my life that I could remember. But it wasn't much. I had

121

buried most of myself by high school, so by this time I was like an accumulated factual list of myself plastered together like a papier-mâché doll. Kale could see the doll and wanted to see me. I didn't know where to begin to show myself. I didn't know myself other than the things I had done. I was my work. I was a girl whose father had died. I was a girl who didn't go to college. I was a girl on a soap opera. I didn't know there was any other self to be.

Kale told me about a therapist he knew in the city and he highly recommended him to me if I ever felt like seeing what might be trapped inside the doll. The mere suggestion of it scared the shit out of me, but I had learned to trust Kale and thought it might be a good idea if he thought it could help me regain some of my lost memory. I hated not knowing who I was. I could barely remember anything before my father's death, and that had only been five years earlier. I thought there was something wrong with me, something terribly wrong with me that was making me forget. I saw my past like line drawings you make as a kid. A sketch of a house, a bus ride, a flame, a Christmas tree, a letter, a mansion, a car, a missing car, a sigh. A purse. A sigh.

I rang the doorbell of a prewar building on the Upper West Side, ten blocks away from where I had moved after my sublet ran out. I felt comfortable in the area and comfortable on the show; I figured it was time to get comfortable with myself. The doorman took me up in the elevator to Dr. Ernst's apartment. When I knocked on the door a man in his early sixties answered and sweetly smiled at me. I had never thought to ask Kale what he looked like and was surprised by how comfortable I felt having a man old enough to be my grandfather asking me to come in. He led me into an office off a waiting room with a couple of chairs in it. No one was sitting in them, which I was glad about. His apartment was off to the other side, behind the closed doors, where I imagined he probably had some cats. His office was simple: a chair where he sat (I could tell because there was a table with a tablet and pen next to it) and another chair that was caramel-colored leather that looked like an easy chair with an ottoman in front of it. There was also a couchlike thing that had no back, so it was more like a bed. A twin-size bed. Over the bed there was a picture of the ocean and sky, and I wondered what it meant to him or if it meant anything at all as he motioned for me to sit down in the caramel.

I sank softly into the chair and noticed he had slippers on his feet as he sat down. Why not wear slippers all day when you work in your house? I would wear slippers, I thought to myself. Slippers are comfortable. I thought it was strange that I didn't own slippers.

Dr. Ernst was the most gentle-looking person I had ever seen. His demeanor was kind and his eyes wrinkled when he looked at me, like he was looking carefully and with caution. He was tender and curious. We sat and looked at each other for a while before anyone spoke. I was not used to silence. Silence made me quite uncomfortable when there were other people around me, and I was used to filling it with a whole bunch of nothing.

"I don't know why I'm here, really. I mean, I guess I kind of do because I don't remember anything about my childhood other than the fact that I could fly down the steps which is kind of weird and I'd kind of like to know why I can't remember anything other than that but I'm fine. I mean, I have a great job, well . . . of course you know that because I'm here because of Kale and he probably told you that I was coming and he knew me from the show—duh! But it's great to be on the show. I like the show. And I really like Kale. He's like the first really good friend that I've ever had. Oh, that's another thing. I don't really have any friends; I never really made any after a while. But I made them up. I made up my friends, but not like in a crazy way, we would just play detective together sometimes. So . . . why do I think I'm here, is that what you asked?"

"I didn't ask anything yet, but I'd like to know." He'd like to know and I'd like to know.

"I'd like to know too," I said.

"Why do you think you might be here other than having no memory except flying down steps and making up friends?"

"Did you get that from what I just said? Did I say all that?"

"Yes."

"Do you think there's something wrong with me?"

"It doesn't look like there's anything wrong with you. What do you mean by something wrong with you?"

"Like *wrong* with me." I thought if I pronounced the word a little clearer, he would get what I meant by it.

"Do you think that there's something wrong with you? Is that why you're here?"

"Well, I think it's a little odd that I can't remember my childhood, and that disturbs me a bit."

"Can you tell me what you *do* remember?"

That I could. I told him the same factual list that I had told Kale. My list usually started with the fact that my father was dead and what he was dead of, and then I went on from there about living in a one-bedroom apartment with my mother and her crying all the time about Nathan and the fact that I hadn't cried about Nathan or my dad or— "Oh, yeah. I think there may be something to that. I never really cried about them being dead."

"Why do you think you haven't cried?"

"Because my mother was crying all the time about it and I didn't have the time. There were enough tears being shed in our house."

"Do you feel like crying about it?"

"I don't think so. But maybe I should, you know? Why wouldn't I feel like crying?"

"You tell me."

"I mean . . . I guess I feel like crying." I didn't know. This was all so confusing. I was talking and words were coming out of my mouth, but I didn't really know what I was saying or what I was feeling about what I was saying.

"I don't know what I feel like doing, to tell you the truth. Maybe I should figure it out and come back."

"You can figure it out in here, if you want some help. That's what I'm here for, Anne. To help you."

Well, I had never thought of that before. Someone helping me? "I guess *that's* why I'm here, huh? Duh."

"What's the duh about?"

"Well, duh, it's so stupid. I guess I'm here to get help."

"That's not stupid. We all need help."

"Oh, well, thanks. I guess I'm here because I need help."

"Well, good. That's what I'm here to give."

I was saying that I needed help, but I didn't even know what for or how much I would need. "I might need a lot."

"I can give a lot. I have an endless supply."

"As long as I pay, you help, right?" Now I was frustrated that I had to pay for help.

"Do you have an issue with paying to get help?" he asked.

"I guess not. No one else was going to do it for free." He was not disturbed by my sarcasm.

"You get paid to do your job because you're good at it, right?"

"Right."

"I get paid for my job because I'm good at it. My job is to give help. If at any time you don't think I'm doing my job well, you can stop paying me. Deal?"

That all sounded logical, and for some reason I was feeling better than when I walked in the door. "Deal."

"So you want to meet next week?"

I did. I made a date and wrote it in my book. Then I canceled the date. Clearly I was afraid of the date. It took me about three weeks to get back in the office and get some help about why I had canceled the date and the next two dates after that. We discovered that it wasn't keeping a date that I was afraid of, I was afraid to get help.

• • •

"You look beautiful with no makeup on."

Did I lose my hearing? Was someone telling me that I looked good without makeup on?

Nick was a bad boy. He drank, he smoked, he stayed out late—everything I wanted in a man. And God, was he *hot*. He wore leather and Levi's and didn't comb his hair and smelled of bar food and girls.

"Did I just hear you say what I thought I heard you say?" I said.

"What do you think you heard me say?"

"Oh, please don't make me play that game."

"You started it. You heard me and then you asked if you heard me. I was only playing what you were playing."

"Yeah, I guess you're right. I'm glad you like me without makeup."

"What, you've never heard that before? Come on, I don't believe that."

I rambled out the story about getting makeup for Christmas when I was little. I was making progress with Dr. Ernst and things were flooding back about my insecurities and why I had so many of them.

"That's awful. You're beautiful," he said.

"Thanks. You're beautiful," I said. He had to know how beautiful he was. I couldn't believe I was flirting with him, he was so beautiful. So beautiful and bad. Bad and beautiful. If I had a type, which I obviously didn't, it would be him.

I was eighteen and although I'd done some pretty stupid things sexually in high school, I was lame in the sexy department. Acting out your idea of sexuality and feeling like a healthy, sensual, sexual being are two completely different things. I was like an awkward toad feeling my way through a pond of murky water. I was lost on how to be a woman. I wasn't a woman. I was a girl acting like a woman. I lived alone and had a job and was on a TV show and going to therapy, but I was A MESS! Just this guy telling me he thought I was beautiful made me quiver all over. I could hardly stand up when he asked me out for a drink. I wasn't old enough to drink!

Of course I said yes. Of course we got drunk. Of course we went to bed. Of course we moved in together. I didn't know that Nick was more than ten years older than me, and even if I had, it wouldn't have mattered. An older man felt more natural than unnatural to me. A guy with a screwy childhood who doused his pain with alcohol felt all the more safe. I was safe in the arms of unsafe things.

He was unstable, I was unstable. He drowned himself in alcohol, I drowned myself in work. He was hiding and I was hiding and we neither one knew how to stop hiding.

Sure, I was in therapy, but for two months. I had years to go on this thing called a healing path. I was just starting to be able to cry, for Pete's sake, and I didn't know what the tears were for. Were they for my father? My brother? Me? My mother? My sisters? I couldn't pinpoint sadness as an emotion let alone all the other ones that were stored up inside me. Emotions scared the daylights out of me. I knew they were there and that they had names, but other than that I was lost.

When you're lost you find lost. That's the rule, I've discovered. You get what you are in relationships. If you don't have yourself together, you'll find someone else who doesn't either. That's what makes us comfortable, so we attract it. There's a term for this. It's called the codependent relationship game. If you're unhealthy and trying to figure out shit with your parents, you'll find someone who's doing the same thing. You'll get the parent you're trying to work your stuff out with. And it's always a two-way street. I chose Nick and Nick chose me. I was looking for someone to save me from the hell with my father and found myself an alcoholic. Hello, Daddy. He was looking for a woman to save him from the torture of his alcoholic father and found a workaholic. Hello, Mommy. Sure, we came in different packages—that's how you get hooked.

My father didn't drink. Nick's mother wasn't a career woman. They had different shields that hid their pain. We all have our shields. We have inherited the need for them from our parents. We attract people who reflect our shields back to us until we have the courage to take down the shields and look at the truth of who we are without them. Some of us do it faster than others. Some of us don't do it at all. Some of us have smaller shields. But until we do the work on ourselves to take down our own, we will not find another person without one. It is only without a shield that we can find true love.

• • •

Anna was walking down the hall like a second finale of a fireworks display on the Fourth of July. She was a dark-haired, dark-eyed beauty and she was heading my way. I had heard about her from Kale, a real *whippet,* he had said, and—"One of the best actresses to grace the show, hands down."

She had gone out to try her luck in LA but it hadn't gone her way. So now she was back to play the character she had created years before, Donna Love. Vicky and Marley's mother. She couldn't have looked more different from either one of the two of me. I could only wish. She breathed exotic and I wanted to be exotic. My plain hair and skin were not yet something I inhabited with pride. I wanted someone else's skin, and I wouldn't have minded at all if it were hers.

"You must be Annie!" she shouted from afar. Her smile beamed in my direction. I was her first stop back at the studio. She wanted to meet this chick playing her twin daughters and size her up a bit. We were both sizing.

"You must be Anna!" I shouted back.

She was carrying bags of stuff that were overflowing and practically spilling out onto the floor in her wake. I assumed it was for her dressing room. I hadn't even thought of making my dressing room my own. She had a lamp sticking out of one bag and something that looked like a statue in another, and before I could see what else, the bags were dropped at her sides and her arms were around me.

"I can't wait to work with you. I've been watching. You're the best Vicky/Marley this show's had."

There had been two before me, and one had won an Emmy. That's the way soaps work. When someone wants off the show or a contract runs out, they get a replacement. I was a replacement and in the beginning was constantly compared to the other girl. But now the roles were mine. The fans had switched their allegiance, and Anna was telling me she had switched hers.

"I hear you're the *only* Donna this show's had. I'm so excited to be working with you." There had been a few actresses that tried to take over the Donna Love character, but no one liked any of them as much as Anna. She was somewhat of a legend.

"Don't listen to anything they say. Haven't you realized it's all bullshit yet?"

Before I could answer she was on to the next and asked, "Is this your dressing room?" She butted past me and looked inside the cement walls and found nothing that made it look like mine, or anyone else's for that matter. "How can you live like this?"

I had never thought about it like that, but living really was what I did there. I was at the studio way more than I was at home.

"It's so drab, for God's sakes, girl. You like living like a depressed hermit? Where did you come from to want to live like this? Yuck."

She was bold. Honest. Hilarious in her inability to hold back what she felt. She pulled her bags into the room and had a seat. "You want some lunch? Have you eaten?"

I hadn't. Hidden underneath what could have been wallpaper for all I knew was a whole barbecued chicken and a loaf of bread. I wouldn't have been surprised if she pulled out a picnic table and four chairs.

"This room is bigger than any room I ever got here. They must like you or be kissing your ass. Sit down."

She was telling me to sit down in my own room. She handed me a napkin and then reached inside her sweater and pulled out her shoulder pads. "Have you learned that trick yet? Under the bra straps? Makes you look ten years younger."

I hadn't learned that trick; I *was* ten years younger.

"You can use your fingers. Who needs utensils anyway?" She pushed the chicken toward me. She dug in and I dug in and she talked and I listened and I talked and she listened and she never left my room. I had another roommate after all, but this time by choice.

For the three years we were on the show together we would never stop talking. No topic was off limits. We dove into obscurity like seagulls into water.

"What do you mean, you don't masturbate? What girl doesn't masturbate?" Well . . . this girl apparently. I hadn't thought about it before. Nick and I had sex a lot, and although I had never had an orgasm, I never thought much about it—and I certainly didn't think about taking the matter into my own hands, if you will. Anna was horrified.

"You've got to learn, sweetie. They can't do it for you, if you can't do it for yourself."

Our conversations were our way of getting through the long days and stressful hours. We would go into our dressing room, she would buy food, and we would talk by the light of her lamp until we had to go back to work. If we were in the middle of a conversation, we would make mental notes and resume where we left off at the next break or the next day, it didn't matter to us. Our friendship had become one long unending conversation about sex and men and women and heroes and heroines and fathers and mothers. It all seemed to weave its way gently together like a soft quilt. The itchy, uncomfortable blankets of my past were slowly coming off in therapy, and Anna was helping me replace them with silky threads of love and honesty and clarity and silliness and kindness and humor and did I mention love? There was so much love.

One day I showed up and there was a package waiting for me, all tied with ribbon in front of my dressing-room mirror. Anna wasn't in the room, but the package beckoned for me to open it. I unwrapped the present and could not believe my eyes. It was a back massager/vibrator with a note in Anna's writing:

ENJOY YOURSELF! LOVE, ANNA

Just as any other girl completely out of touch with her body might do, I took the vibrator home and hid it in my closet. I waited until Nick was at the gym one Saturday and pulled it down from the shelf where I had hidden it between sweaters way in the back. I went into the bathroom, locked the door, and climbed into the shower. After being fully washed and scrubbed—I believed my body to be a dirty thing to touch—I wrapped a towel around myself, plugged the vibrator into a socket, and lay back on the cold tile floor to be charged with all the goodness that I felt masturbation had to offer.

My backbone got raw rubbing on the tile floor, my feet slid into the side of the tub and got bruised, my elbows sloshed around trying to find security while slipping on the puddles left from the shower—and my vagina? My vagina had no idea what hit it. I felt an electric shock shoot through me that could have been because the vibrator was plugged into a socket with water in it, or because vibrators are meant to feel like electric shocks. Either way, I was off the floor in a flash, hiding the scary thing back in the closet and returning to my blissful state of vaginal ignorance. I immediately instated a new policy in my life called *My vagina? What vagina?* And thought of a new title for a Dr. Seuss book called *I Do Not See a Vagina There. I Do Not See a Vagina Anywhere.*

• • •

Nick and I had been living together for about one year by now and going codependent was working quite well for us. Because of a dwindling bank account and no job, Nick convinced me that he couldn't live in the city anymore. His solution was to move back to his hometown in suburbia where he could reconnect with his high school buddies. Like a good codependent, I packed up the few things I had, put my dog in the backseat of a red Volvo station wagon I bought for the very occasion, and zoomed off to a place called "Inconvenient." I would now be embarking on a two-and-a-half-hour commute to work every day while Nick banged on his drum set.

We had a lovely apartment on the bottom floor of a house with a backyard for our two dogs to run around in. Not that I would be seeing very much of the dogs, or Nick for that matter. I was spending at least twelve hours a day at the studio by this point, and memorizing at least forty pages of dialogue a night. Playing twins is the hardest job I have ever had. When you're young they take advantage of you, and I was in the habit of being taken advantage of, so it didn't bother me. I was a pro. I hid behind the twins so much I was the twins. When things got tough with Nick, I held my job as my priority. It became very hard to communicate with so little time together, and although we kept up a facade that everything was okay, everything was not okay.

I got nominated for an Emmy my first year on the show, and when Nick told me that he couldn't go to the awards because he had a job interview, I smiled at the lack of support and cut off all my hair. I thought that this was what you put up with in adult relationships. I could take care of myself, that had been proven. I didn't need anyone to take care of me.

When I got pregnant at nineteen (we Christians didn't believe in birth control), I knew I had to get an abortion. Christians don't believe in abortions any more than they believe in birth control, so I couldn't call my mother for help. She was still judging me for moving in with a man out of wedlock anyway. I couldn't tell anyone on the soap because I was afraid I would get fired, so I hid my little secret for five weeks from everyone except Nick and a close friend of mine. When Nick had another job interview the day of my abortion, she picked me up at the doctor's office, tucked me in bed, and returned to work. When Nick didn't arrive home until the next day from his interview, he wondered why I was upset. "You want me to get a job, don't you? You *don't* want me to be like your *daddy,* do you?"

Nick had a convenient way of blaming every problem I had with him on my father. I was just beginning to deal with my anger in therapy. Memory was coming back and I would share my discoveries about my dad with Nick, who would support me when I told him and then throw them back in my face like weapons when we had arguments. I didn't want to lose Nick, so I would back down and agree with him. I considered my mother's relationship with my father a failure, and I wasn't going to fail like my mother. The parallels of communication and lack thereof were too close for me to see. I didn't know that putting up with Nick's manipulations and drinking and lack of support and fighting was just putting up with another form of abuse. I wanted to be good at love, I really did. I just didn't know how. I didn't know that to be good at love you had to love yourself first.

FRESNO, 2000

"You can keep my credit card. I won't need it where I'm goin'." I had never felt so good.

"You sure?" The dude behind the counter had never felt so confused.

"I'm sure." I turned to go, leaving the gas station attendant with my Visa. I was sorry I didn't have my Amex to give him as well, but it was in my car and I figured I could throw it out the window on my way to the spaceship.

"Hey, lady, I'm not so sure about this."

"You don't need to be sure. I'm sure enough for both of us. You'll see."

"What do you mean I'll see?"

"When I get there, you'll know."

"Get where?"

"Where I'm going."

"Where's that?"

"You'll see, I told ya. If I tell you now, it'll ruin the surprise."

"What surprise?"

"The surprise about where I'm goin'."

"Well, won't you need this wherever it is?" He held up my Visa again like I had forgotten it was a credit card and at closer glance I would see my mistake and take it back.

"You don't need credit cards where I'm goin'. So I'm leavin' it behind. With you."

"I don't get it. Is this some kind of joke?"

"No joke, buddy. I wouldn't kid about somethin' like this."

I skipped out to my four-wheel drive. It was about a hundred and five degrees where I was, and I was out. Out in the middle of nowhere-that-I-knew, to be exact. I had been led there. I had been told to turn up the five freeway to get there. So I turned. I had never been up the five freeway and now I knew why. It was dusty and dry and fucking hot. Nothing but fields of dirt as far as the eye could see. Fields of dirt.

I took off my shirt to wipe my brow before getting back into my truck. I was going to put it back on when I heard it again clear as a bell: "What are you doin' that for? There's no shame in heaven. Keep your shirt off."

With my tank on empty and my heart filled with love, I peeled out of the station and left the dude in my dust.

> *This world is not my home. I'm just a-passin' through.*
> *If heaven's not my home, then Lord, what would I do?*
> *The angels beckon me from heaven's open door,*
> *And I can't feel at home in this world anymore.*

• • •

It was my twentieth birthday and Nick said he had a surprise for me. I was to get dressed up in my fanciest of fancy before I left for work so that I was dressed for the occasion. He was going to pick me up at the studio and take me out someplace that I couldn't possibly guess.

All day I was excited. Only one of the twins was working that day by complete accident, so I was going to be off work by midafternoon, a rare occurrence. When they called *cut!* on the last of my scenes, I tore up to my dressing room, got dressed, and ran outside to where Nick was waiting at the curb in a cab. We drove hand in hand into the city, with Nick taunting me the whole way about his surprise. When we pulled up to the heliport on the West Side of Manhattan, you bet your ass I was shocked. Nick had rented a helicopter to take me up and see the city from above. We loaded into the chopper just as the sun was about to set and took off into the gorgeous night sky. We flew all the way to Brooklyn to see over the studio and back around to see the glory of the glistening Manhattan skyline. Nothing could've been more beautiful.

When we were circling right above the head of the Statue of Liberty, Nick reached into his breast pocket and started saying something over the noise of the beating rotors.

"What?" I couldn't hear him. He looked like he was trying to be romantic, but it was impossible to be romantic and be heard at the same time.

"WILL YOU MARRY ME?"

It couldn't be. I mean, I liked that he was putting such effort into my birthday and all, but marriage? I was only twenty years old, and we fought practically every day now. I decided to delay.

"WHAT?" I yelled again. "I CAN'T HEAR YOU!" I thought maybe he would get cold feet and think of another thing to holler, like *I love you!* or *Nice night, isn't it?* or *Look at her crown, how it sparkles!* But no such luck.

"WILL. YOU. MARRY. ME?" He said it so slow and so loud that I couldn't think it was anything other than what it *exactly* was. A proposal. Each syllable was so clearly enunciated it fell on my ears like molasses. I thought I was *in* molasses.

How do you tell a man in a chopper that you don't want to marry him? He went through all this trouble. He thought it through so clearly. He spent all this *money*. He was showing me he cared, and isn't that all a woman wants? We were flying over the Statue of Liberty at sunset in a hunk of sky-chopping metal for God's sake! He proposed to me over the Statue of Liberty. How do you tell a man that you want *liberty* when you're flying over *liberty* being asked to give your *liberty* away? It was all so goddamn ironic I wanted to jump.

"GIVE ME FREEDOM OR GIVE ME DEATH!" I wanted to scream. But I didn't dare. I figured I would save my voice and save some time by not saying anything at all and crying instead. I was getting good at crying by now, and tears easily came to the surface. I threw my arms around him and thanked him profusely and from the bottom of my soul. I figured when we landed and the noise of the fucking rotors in my eardrums died down I would get the next idea. But, first, I needed a drink.

When the chopper landed, I had an emerald on my finger. I thought about Amway and how many suds we would've sold.

"LET'S GET A DRINK!" I cheered too loud and grabbed for

my ears. My mother's smile was plastered on my face, and I wanted to drink it off as fast as possible.

A cab dropped us in front of our favorite Scandinavian hideout where we liked to eat beef borscht and sausages. The romance of it all was too much. We walked through the door into the cavernous eatery and—"SURPRISE!"

Holy fuck. Every single person I had ever met was standing with schnapps raised to congratulate me on the engagement! When I saw my mother dancing toward me, it was me that I heard.

SQUEAK! I was squeaking! Oh, no!

SQUEAK! Squeak, squeak, SQUEAK! My arms were around his neck and I was most certainly trying to choke him to death.

"OH! OH! OH! THIS IS UNBELIEVABLE. OH NICK! THANK YOU! THANK YOU, NICK, THANK YOU! THANK YOU!" *THANK YOU FOR MY TRIP TO RUSSIA!*

• • •

"Help! Help! The sky is falling! The sky is falling."

Dr. Ernst knew about all my problems with Nick, but like any good therapist couldn't tell me to get the fuck out. Instead he told me to get on the couch.

The couch was where Dr. Ernst and I did most of our work. He was a Reichian therapist. I'll describe that as clearly as I can so that you get the idea of what our work was about, but please understand that all therapists are different. I'm not recommending anything here; I'm just telling you what I did. The idea behind this therapy is that people store emotions in their bodies. When a child is hurt and unable to express it, she or he keeps it inside, therefore forming a sort of pocket around the emotion like a storage container. Sometimes, along with the emotion, the child can store the action or memory of the action in this pocket. Once you are an adult, these pockets are still inside of you, and if the emotion can be released, so then can the memory.

Remember please that I am only speaking for myself. I am not speaking for all cases. The work that Dr. Ernst and I did together was getting into the pockets, releasing the emotion, and discovering the truth of what was hidden inside me. This process was how I regained some of the memory of my childhood. Dr. Ernst called it "bodywork." For the record, these are *my* memories. I have no way to prove what happened to me; that's one of the reasons abuse is so hard to talk about. I did not walk around with a tape recorder, I have no snapshots of these events, I have my memory, and I am as confident as I can be without proof that my story happened the way I am telling it.

Bodywork consisted of the patient, me in this case, getting on the couch in a comfortable position, usually on my back, while Dr. Ernst sat at my side in his chair. I would get as relaxed as possible. Slowly, Dr. Ernst would touch different pressure points in my body where emotions are stored, not unlike what a massage therapist does during intensive treatment. If the point was particularly painful to me, it was clear that I had stored emotion there, and he would gently add pressure to release what was inside. After the emotion was released, he would ask me to tell him the first thing that came to mind. These steps, taken week after week, month after month, slowly brought my memory back.

I'll be honest with you: This was not fun. Healing yourself can be kind of fun sometimes, because you are confronting yourself and learning about who you are from the inside, but I can't say these sessions were fun for me. The first time I got on the couch was three months into my therapy. Dr. Ernst lightly put his hand on the upper part of my chest where my throat and collarbone connect, and I could barely breathe because I began sobbing so hard.

Immediately I remembered trying to scream as a child, but I didn't know about what. That would take time.

Another time Dr. Ernst pressed pressure points in my arms and hands. My body memory came back with such intensity that I started beating at him with my fists and went into a complete and utter panic attack in his office. I left with blotchy spots all over my body and my face because I had been screaming so hard.

My body remembered my abuse before my brain. I had pockets

of sadness and anger, yes, but I had stored my fight, my physical fight that I fought each time I was abused. As young as I was, I had no chance of beating off my father, but I sure as hell tried. I tried everything, and each one of my efforts was explored in the safety of Dr. Ernst's office.

Sometimes I would lie dead, utterly devoid of emotion. Sometimes I would curl into a fetal position and weep quietly. Sometimes I would choke violently and spit up. Sometimes I would scream bloody murder. Sometimes I would hit the couch with my fists until I was too tired to move.

When you are abused you try every kind of defense you can conjure. None of them works, so you stop trying and start storing. Dr. Ernst and I worked on and off for three years, unblocking and releasing, discovering and weeping.

"You need a break, Anne."

Dr. Ernst was sitting in his chair, I in mine. "You've done so much work here about your father. You need to take what you've learned and apply it in the world. I can't be your only safety."

I couldn't hold back how sad and confused I was. "But I've come so far. I thought I was doing so well."

"Yes. You are. You have. And you need a break. There's other work to be done with your father, and you haven't begun to confront your feelings about your mother. She's going to be harder for you."

"Harder? How could anything be harder than this? What are you talking about?"

"She didn't stop the abuse, Anne. She was there the whole time and didn't stop it."

"I know that, but I still don't understand."

"The issues with your father are closer to the surface, easier to define. He did horrible things to you and then he died. But your mother stood by him the whole time. She didn't hear you. You needed to be heard. She didn't rescue you. You needed to be rescued."

I had never thought about the role my mother played. "Why didn't my mother save me?"

"I don't know the answer to that question, Anne."

I was more curious than angry at that point. The anger would come later.

"Allow yourself to take a break. She's not going anywhere, and you need to care for yourself, what you've learned and how much you've accomplished here. This is a long road you are traveling—you need to be patient with yourself."

I rose to go. I always knew when it was time to leave. Dr. Ernst met me at the door as he always did. We looked at each other for a while and then hesitantly I asked him for a hug. I had never hugged him before. He had never tried to hug me. Without any words he gently put his arms around me. "Take care of yourself. Call me if you need me."

• • •

I think I felt abandoned by Dr. Ernst even though he was trying to help me. I had put all of my trust in him, but I didn't trust him enough to tell him how I really felt. I felt like I was a walking heap of mess. I didn't know whom to trust, especially not myself, and I was afraid to tell him that. I was afraid to tell him that I wasn't ready to leave, because I wanted to be good at therapy. I wanted to think that I could handle things on my own. I wanted to be a good patient and take what I had learned into the world. But I wasn't really sure what I had learned, to be honest. I had learned that a lot of terrible things had happened to me. I had learned that my body was filled with disgusting and gross things that my father put into me, and although I had screamed and hollered and cried and fought, I didn't know what to do with that information. I couldn't even look at myself naked, I hated myself so much. My body was ugly to me, so ugly I couldn't touch it. I couldn't respond with pleasure when someone else touched it. But I pretended that I enjoyed it. I was good at pretending. I was so good, I didn't even think of it as pretending. I thought of it as my duty, and I thought every woman felt the same way I did about sex.

I knew that I had to get out of my relationship with Nick, so I did. My mother and I moved me out of our house one night when he was away on business. The fighting had gotten to be so bad that I couldn't even tell him that I was leaving. I found an apartment and moved into it behind his back. It was all so secretive and ugly. I needed out, but the way I got out was slimy and untruthful. I was scared. Scared of him and scared of myself. When I got scared I hid, and I had two ways to do that: dive into work and dive into unhealthy sexual relationships. I did both.

As my patterns have shown, I was comfortable with older men. Sam was older. He was strikingly handsome with thick, salt-and-pepper hair, and he played guitar and had cats. He represented calm. He was in AA and that seemed healthy and opposite of what I had been living with. He was kind to me always. There was nothing about our sex that was abusive in any way; it was the way we related to each other that reflected our individual unhealthy, unre-solved patterns. That is abusive.

Sam liked younger women, as most men in their forties/almost fifties do who aren't married and don't know why. It makes them feel like they're *not* in their forties/almost fifties. Sam was still wrapped up in his last twenty-something girlfriend when we started fucking. Of course that was perfect for me. Here was a man who was in love with someone else. There was no way he could love me. Get-ting less than what I deserved made me comfortable. I was good at getting less. When I got less, I gave less. Less of myself and more of what I thought whoever I was with wanted.

I tried to be what Nick wanted. I tried to be what Sam wanted. I tried to be what everyone I was with wanted, until I couldn't be it anymore. I wanted to be good enough, pretty enough, sexy enough for him *not* to love who he was really loving, and love *me* instead. This would somehow prove that I was lovable. I would put myself on the back burner for someone and twist and contort myself into what I thought they wanted so that they would love me. In the process, *me* got left at the door, buried in the couch, hung out to dry. I became the *idea* of me that I thought they all wanted.

I would purposefully forget my needs, my wants, my desires

and focus on theirs because I thought that's what love was. I thought I would get love in return. But not being yourself only gets you away from love. Not being yourself never gets you the love you deserve, because you deserve to be loved for you, who you are, what you want and desire. Any form of love you receive when who you really are is not in the picture is not going to feel like love. In fact, it will feel like the opposite of love. It's going to feel like abuse. In fact, you are abusing yourself. You are giving yourself less than what you deserve, and that is abusive to yourself. You are the responsible party once you become an adult. It is your responsibility to recognize where you are in a relationship, and if it doesn't feel good, you are right. If it feels weird, it is weird. But the other person in the relationship is not responsible. You are. I didn't know that then, I know that now. I would accept less and less, contort more and more for the next eight years of my life, until I figured out this pattern and started being me in the relationship.

Yes, I needed more therapy. Yes, I got more therapy. Yes, my inability to see me clearly was tied up in the pain of my abusive family. Yes, I wanted love from my mother and father. Yes, it wasn't given to me. Yes, I would do anything and everything to get it. Yes, I would try to get it from others. Yes, I went out and slept with substitutes for my mother and my father. Yes, it would always leave me wounded and disappointed. Yes, it was unbearable. Yes, it was painful. Yes, I did drugs to cover the pain. Yes, I had sex to cover the pain. Yes, I hid my pain in my fame. Yes, my patterns drove me crazy. Yes, I went crazy.

I went so crazy trying to get love and not getting it that I created an entirely different personality that didn't need love at all. Not getting love drove me crazy. I wasn't crazy for wanting love; no one is crazy for wanting love. I went to the ends of the earth to get it, literally, and I found it. And you know who I found it in? Me. I found love in me. After I found love in me, I was able to find love in others.

• • •

As my popularity rose the longer I was on *Another World,* I began to question what I wanted to do with my life. I had heard the horror stories about people who had tried to make it in LA. The perceived insignificance of soap opera acting wasn't lost on me. I had had the best four years of my life playing these twins. I had met friends whom I would cherish forever. But I didn't want to make a career of being a soap actress and was too afraid to commit to being a "real" actress without a job in place.

I had developed a passion for architecture and design (perhaps I was my father's daughter) and decided to apply to Parsons School of Design. I had seen the soap years as college years and thought that the New School would be like graduate school for me. I began talking about it around the halls of the studio, and everyone told me I should at least give LA a shot. I had recently signed with an agent, so why not see what she could do for me before making any rash decisions?

I applied to school, just to be safe, and was accepted. I had about three weeks left to go on the show and it looked like my career path had been decided when I got a call from my agent.

"I know we're getting close to the deadline of school, but I got an audition for you. I think you'll like it." She explained that a company called Hallmark Hall of Fame was doing a TV movie of the Willa Cather novel *O Pioneers!* They wanted me to audition to play Jessica Lange's best friend in the movie.

"You've got to be kidding."

"No, why? You read the book?"

"I just finished it last week. It's sitting here right in front of me."

One of my favorite producers on the soap had given me Cather's novels because she thought I would enjoy the writing. I picked *O Pioneers!* to read first and loved it. I took the call as another sign from God about the direction in my life and decided that if I got the part, I would take it instead of going to school. I certainly wasn't stupid enough to pass up the opportunity to work with Jessica Lange, if that's what God wanted me to do. I loved her work. I didn't really have an idol, but if I had, she would have been it.

I guess you know the ending to this story. I'm not writing a book on the ins and outs of architecture, although in a way I am writing a book on how I built my life. When I met Jessica and asked her about how she approached her characters, she said she did it from the outside in. She got the clothes and the wig right so she could look at herself as the character, and then step by step she would build the emotional interior. I guess that's a description of where I was at this stage in my life. The exterior of me was starting to find its shape, make its mold. I was an actress. I was a person dedicated to healing my life. I had good, solid friendships to help guide my way and a therapist and healer who had laid the foundation for me in my journey toward self-love. I was ready to start building my emotional interior.

CHAPTER TEN

DRUGS AND
OTHER DISTRACTIONS

When I arrived in LA I had a dog by my side, an Emmy in my trunk, and a phone number in my pocket. I had won the Emmy while on a bed at a Motel 6 in a town not worth remembering in Nebraska. When they called my name I celebrated by clearing my greasy burger off my bed to find the phone.

"Hello?"

"Congratulations!" It was my agent.

"Thanks, Joanne. Thanks."

"Are you thrilled?"

"Sure. I only wish shooting a movie was as glamorous as they made it sound when they said I wasn't there."

"Not so glamorous, huh?"

"Who's complaining? Hey, listen, does this mean I'm an actress?"

"I think it does."

"So will I have to go to LA at some point, if I wanna do it for real?"

"At some point, yeah."

"Okay. I'll move to LA."

"No rush, Anne."

"No rush."

I packed up my apartment two days after the shoot was over and was in my car a day after that. I don't like to waste time when something has to be done. If it has to be done, do it. Nick was in LA while I was shooting with "Jess" in the cornfields. We had broken up and broken up again and were still trying to figure out if we were broken up when I called him to help me find an apartment. He did. Again the confusion about being broken up came up.

"So are we . . . ?"

"Who knows."

"I don't know. Things were so fucked-up for a while."

"Things were always fucked-up, Anne. I was fucked-up and you were fucked-up." We were so eloquent and so fucked-up.

"I've been doing a lot of work on myself since I've been here."

"Really? That's great."

"Yeah. It feels great."

"You look great; it shows."

"You look great."

We talked and fucked and talked some more about why we were fucking and why we seemed to be connecting better than we'd been before. "This new therapy that I'm trying really seems to be helping me break through some stuff in a way I couldn't before," he said.

I was intrigued. "Really? What is it?"

He was hesitant. "I'm doing LSD therapy."

I had taken LSD one night at a Grateful Dead concert and had the time of my life. It was just that I could barely remember what time that was so I didn't do it again. To be quite frank, drugs scared me. The idea that they could help me, however, fascinated me.

Nick explained all about the therapy and the sixties and Timothy Leary and how LSD had benefited his life and the lives of many others whom he knew. It was all strange and curious, and I wanted to meet these others. Nick introduced me to a group of his friends who were also doing this radical therapy, and they all told me how much it had helped them. (Incidentally, Nick's hard work paid off—I heard he stopped drinking.) These people were among the most loving, giving, honest, straightforward I had met. I liked what they were telling me; it sounded very similar to what Dr. Ernst and I had been doing in New York, but without the drug. I wanted to know more.

As it was described to me, a very low dose of LSD could take you into your unconscious mind and allow you to see what is stored there. Like Dr. Ernst's emotional storage bins, once discovered, the pain could be released. These "journeys" would take place with a therapist who would help guide you. The LSD worked as a tool, not as a solution, to allow you to see yourself in a clearer and deeper way by allowing you to release the emotional blocks of your childhood. I was intrigued. But I didn't want to do this therapy alone. If I was going to be exploring something this intense and potentially scary, I wanted another therapist not involved in this "journey work" to help me too.

After getting settled in an apartment and taking a break as Dr. Ernst had suggested, I found another Reichian therapist. I picked a woman this time because I wanted a strong female presence to guide me in dealing with my relationship with my mother. I told Dr. Mann about my life and the work I had done with Dr. Ernst. I told her what I thought my issues were with my family and mother and what I was ready to confront and heal in this next stage of therapy. I also told her about the LSD therapy I was considering and wanted her opinion.

She had heard of LSD therapy. She had also heard of its being incredibly helpful and healing. Although she could not recommend it to me (LSD *is* illegal), she agreed that she would work with me knowing that I was also exploring this other therapeutic avenue for healing.

Don't get me wrong, LSD is illegal and so is the "work" that I am about to describe. I *do not* recommend this type of therapy or drug use to anyone. I am telling you about it because it was an important tool that helped me heal my life.

I had two long conversations with Arthur over the phone before I met him. Although we were talking about an illegal form of therapy, the conversations were very much like the beginning conversations with any therapist. He asked me questions about my life, what I wanted to explore, what I thought my blocks and issues were. He told me about himself and why he did this work and how he felt it helped people. He had a sweet, calm voice. He neither encouraged nor discouraged me from doing this journey work. He talked about the growth he had seen in other patients, but was clear with me that this work wasn't for everyone. He warned that it could get scary at times and perhaps take me to places within my mind that could get uncomfortable both physically and mentally. He explained that some people hadn't liked the intensity, but he had never encountered any problems with a client and no one had ever been hurt while working with him. He was very honest about the fact that I would be taking a drug, an illegal substance, and that I was responsible for that decision. He explained that he had been doing this work since the sixties and used theories very similar to what Timothy Leary describes in his books, and he recommended that I read them. He described the process to me over the phone and told me that he would explain anything I had questions about in further detail at any time. He understood that making this commitment was a big one and that I needed to be clear about it. After deep contemplation over the next couple of months, I made my decision.

• • •

A couple I met through Nick had become very good friends of mine. They offered to drive me to my session and pick me up afterward. The first time was always scary and very emotional, they explained, and they wanted to show me their support. We showed up at Arthur's house at nine o'clock on a Saturday morning. He had told me to wear comfortable clothing. I would be lying on a bed all day and wanted to be flexible. We had talked about my sessions with Dr. Ernst and he explained that similar body reactions could happen and I should be prepared. When he opened the door he had a smile on his face and a glass of orange juice in his hand.

He was sweeter and smaller than I had imagined, with an Asian beauty I found immediately appealing. My friends hugged him and then said good-bye to us, wishing me a good journey and love in my travels into the mind. Arthur and I talked for a while and he soothed my nervous energy before getting started.

"It's always scary the first time," he said. "After that it's always easier."

I didn't know if there would be a second time, and I told him so.

"It's up to you, Annie. Every choice you make is yours."

That was a refreshing thought. Every choice is mine? I had never thought of that before, but it sounded so obvious. I had made my choice. I was there. I wanted the journey.

"I'm ready," I said.

He took my hand and said a quick prayer: "God, goddess, all that is . . . make this a safe journey for Anne and let her know that I will be here to help and guide her when she needs it."

He handed me a little pill and a glass of water. After I took it, he led me to a bed and handed me a set of eyeshades and a pair of earphones. To be completely in your unconscious mind, there had to be no outside distractions, he had told me. He would play music as my guide, but discouraged me from taking off the eyeshades at any time unless I needed to use the restroom. If I wanted a sip of water, I could call out and he would bring it to me. If I was scared, he would come to my side. If I felt an emotion, he encouraged me to be with it, allow it, feel it. The work was about feeling and releasing the feeling so you could be free. When I was ready for my journey, I lay down on the bed, covered my eyes, and covered my ears. Soon I heard music and was on my way.

• • •

I have to admit I thought drugs would be fun. I mean, come on, they're drugs! I thought the music would come on and I would sink into a great feeling, maybe feel a rush of pleasure wash over my body and maybe see some fun stuff, like fairies or colorful clowns or anything for that matter before I got into the *me* of it all. I mean, I knew I would get into the me of it all—that's what I was there for. That's what I *paid* for, to see myself in a deeper, clearer way. That's what was promised. But I had no idea what I was in for. The image I saw of myself was the scariest, ugliest, most uncomfortable, disgusting thing I have ever seen. I saw myself as shit. No kidding, no lie. I saw and was shit.

I don't want to gross anyone out. I am not meaning to scare anyone. I am telling you the truth of what I saw and what I felt inside myself. I saw me as shit. I don't know how long it took for the unrecognizable sounds coming through the earphones to guide me to the toilet in my mind, but it couldn't have been long because it's all I remember about the day. First I was looking at my shit in the toilet, then I was my shit. Just like that, every bit of me was shit. And there was nothing I could do about it. I *was* it. Yes, it was all in my mind, but my mind saw shit. I could feel it on me, in me, up me, and around me. I could not escape it. It strangled me. It tortured me. It gagged me.

I had been encouraged to *allow* the feeling. *Explore* the feeling. How do you *allow* a feeling when you ARE the feeling? Shit was coming out of every pore of me. I reeked of it. I was rolling in it when I turned over, and I was sitting in it when I sat up. I was it. I was shitting shit and I was the shit I was shitting.

I was disgusting, absolutely awfully disgustingly disgusting. I was grosser than gross. I couldn't get away from me and how gross I was. I thought to call Arthur over, but what was I going to say? He wanted me to *feel* my feelings. Well, I felt them all right. I was chok-ing on them. What was he going to do with *my* shit? I wanted to do this therapy thing right. I wanted to be *in* my feelings, even if I hated them more than anything I had hated in my life. I wasn't going to take drugs and whine about it all day. If shit was on the plate, I was going to handle shit. I can be shit, I thought. *Surely this shit can't last all day!* Ha! Double ha! It felt like years in that bed of shit and shame and grossness. I felt like the torture was never going to end.

"How ya doin', Annie?"

I heard the sweet voice of Arthur under my earphones and I wanted to kill. I ripped off my shades, got tangled in my ear cord, and started to scream at him. I don't know what the words were. I think I told him something or other about what I saw, how I felt, but I couldn't describe how awful it was. When I was done screaming, the screaming turned to tears. Tears of rage and tears of sadness and tears of complete and utter embarrassment about what I saw, what I felt. When I was done, my body fell limp on the bed like I was dead.

"Who am I? Who the fuck am I? I am nothing. I am nothing. I am shit, Arthur, shit."

"You are not shit, Annie. Nothing about you is shit."

"Then why did I see that? Why was it all over me? Why was I nothing? Why am I so nothing?"

I was a heap of pain and crying and sobbing. I had never felt so low, so ugly, and so utterly embarrassed. Arthur tried to calm me down, holding me and gently explaining what I saw.

"When you are abused, you take on the shame of the person who abused you, and you think that you are the abuse. Your image of the abuse is what you saw. It is *not* you."

"I hate it. I hate it so much. I don't want to be that. I can't be that. How can I live like that?"

"You don't have to live like that. That's why you're here. To see it, feel the pain of it, then let it go. It is not yours. You are *not* your abuse. What happened to you is *not* your fault. What was done to you is in your past, and if you can see what it has made you feel about yourself, you can heal it and let it go. You are not the shit. The shit is the shame of your father—it is not yours. Do you understand the difference?"

I understood the difference, but it felt like mine.

"How do I get it out of me?"

"By experiencing the feelings around it and putting those feelings in the appropriate place outside of yourself. By giving those feelings back to the people who deserve them so that they are not directed at yourself."

Dr. Ernst said it would be a long road, and I was feeling the length of the trip. "Will I ever get out of the shit?"

"Yes, I believe you will. That's what I am here to help you do."

I was feeling so gross that I didn't think I could get off the bed, walk out the door, or ever have my life again. I felt so sorry for myself and anyone else who had ever had the shame of someone else put inside their body. Someone else's shame is so ugly. My father's shame was so ugly.

"I don't want it in me. I want it out of me."

"Knowing that it's not yours is a good place to start."

"I am not my father."

"You are not your father."

"I am not shit." I said it like it was the beginning of my life's mantra.

"You are not shit, Annie. I'm sorry that that happened to you. But you are not your abuse. You are a beautiful person who was abused as a child. You are now an adult, here to see yourself separate from the abuse so you can live happily and fully as you."

It was a nice thought. *To live happily and fully as me.* I would ponder this day for months before I could return to Arthur and the interior of my mind to get my next lesson.

• • •

The easiest way to explain myself during this time is to say that I existed as two people. I was the person who went to therapy and sat on the couch in Dr. Mann's office exploring my feelings of shit and shame, and I was the person who continued to be a workaholic. I fought each day in auditions and readings to become a successful actress. I made a promise to myself that I would be directing my own movies by the time I was twenty-nine. I didn't know that festering underneath my drive was a goal I had unconsciously set for myself to receive the love of my father. I made becoming a successful actress my goal, and I fought each day to attain it. I did whatever it took to win the hearts of casting directors. But I did it through my work, my commitment. I took no shortcuts, kissed no ass. I dressed as the characters when I went in to read. I memorized every line off every side that I got so that I never had to look down at a page in an audition. I learned accents, sang songs, or dyed my hair if that's what a role called for. I didn't believe in being lazy. I believed in fighting a fight and showing that I was competent and capable of anything they asked. I went back two times or ten times, if that's what they wanted. I built my reputation slowly, and I earned every job I got.

The first week I arrived in LA I got a part on *Murphy Brown* playing what they described as a "young Murphy." I loved watching Candice Bergen and admired her for what she had accomplished. But I knew that I wouldn't make it to her level of success by doing guest-starring roles on other people's TV shows, and I made a commitment to myself to never do a guest appearance again. In fact, television was out altogether, I decided, unless it was cable. I told my agent and stayed true to my promise.

Three weeks later I auditioned for a play called *Us and Them,* written and directed by a woman named Betsy Thomas. I was cast to play her. I didn't know anyone when I moved to LA and was all of a sudden surrounded by a group of creative people my own age. That was new for me. I had never had friends my own age. I didn't understand people my own age. They were just starting to get their bearings after graduating from college. They spent their time smoking pot, drinking beer, and playing air guitar. It was so foreign to me I couldn't relate. I had been working since I was twelve, had been on a soap, and had no idea how to relax, kick back, and have a good time. They tried to teach me. I tried to smoke pot. I tried to "hang out," but I couldn't really. They lovingly made fun of me and I of them.

I thought that if I started dating a guy that hung in their circle, I would feel more comfortable, but that didn't work either. Having sex with a guy my own age was more frustrating than not being able to smoke pot. Henry was the most adorable guy I had ever seen. He wore baggy Levi's, brass buckles, and thrift-store jackets. He was the definition of mellow and "cool" in that way that guys whom you want to be friends with in high school are "cool." I had a history that was too ugly to explain to someone just out of college. He was beginning to define his life. He was a writer, a brilliant writer at that, but I was coming to terms with being raped and homeless, and I felt like an outcast. A girl with all this baggage, a burden. The last thing I felt was cool. These people were cool. I could play them in plays, but I wasn't them. At least not to me. I was the opposite of them. They were the *us* and I was the *them*.

As luck would have it, I got an offer to go to North Carolina to act in a TV-movie series of Young Indiana Jones stories. I couldn't believe it, I was going to meet the man who made the very first movie I saw—Mr. George Lucas. I didn't contain my glee at getting parts, I still don't. Every part I get I scream for joy. I feel lucky when I get hired, and when the luck is this good, I jump and shout. Each and every one of my roles I feel I got for a reason. A reason that would shape the rest of my life and lead me to the next place that I was supposed to go—not only in my career. Every single thing that happened in my life happened for a reason, and I mean everything. Without my father, my mother, and my childhood, I wouldn't be where I am today. Without each part, each role, each place I traveled, I wouldn't be writing this book. If I hadn't done the Young Indy series, I wouldn't have met Lindsey. And Lindsey was worth a meet.

There was a layover on the flight from North Carolina to LA and I got off the plane. As I liked to do back then, I played the game of

"Who's the cutest person in the airport?" If you've never played, it's really fun, and it's played exactly like it sounds. You ask yourself who the cutest person in the airport is and then you find them. Well, my eyes were gazing and my mind straying when I came upon a guy in all black. Black from head to toe. Now, we were in the boonies, remember, and not many people were dressed in black. In fact, no one was. We're talking floral and flannel. Black was way too mod in these parts. Of course I had to move closer. I was really curious now because the guy was standing in line for *my* plane. He was really skinny, which also made him stand out, because along with the floral and flannel look these people had goin', they were not turning down cheese and pie at the dinner table, if you know what I mean. He was wearing sunglasses, this guy, so I couldn't really see his eyes, but either way, he got my vote. If not for looks—at least originality.

I got on the plane and lo and behold who was I sitting next to? Mr. Black on black on black himself. I scooted into my first-class seat (I got to sit in first class when a movie company flew me around) and tried not to look under his glasses to see if he was worth the vote. He was paying absolutely *no* attention to me but was fiddling with a cassette player and headphones, which interested me as well. As I was casually looking absolutely nowhere, he plopped a tape down in that middle section between the seats and I casually had to look right at it. It was labeled DRUM TRACKS. What are drum tracks? I wondered, thinking it was obvious, but kind of wanting to know from him.

"Are you a drummer?" I innocently asked as he was readying to put on the earphones.

"Ah . . . no. No, I'm not."

"Oh." I was still curious. "Are you a musician?"

"Ah . . . yes. Yes, I am."

"Neat," I said—and could have popped a lollipop into my mouth. "What do you play?"

"Guitar," he answered simply and sort of smiled, but more like a Mona Lisa kind of a smile, not the real thing.

"Neat."

That got a for-real smile. I guessed he liked the word "neat."

"You ever play with anyone I might have heard of?"

Now he was full-on smiling. I guessed that of course he hadn't. Didn't I see the Podunk town we were flying out of?

"You ever hear of Fleetwood Mac?"

"Fleetwood Mac?" I said it like I had to chew on it. "I don't think so, no. Why, should I have?"

By the way he was looking at me, I thought he thought I should have. "No, not especially."

"I still think it's neat, though. Are you going to LA to try your luck?"

"Something like that, yeah," he said. And then he took off his glasses. He didn't know that I was playing a game, but if he had I would have told him that he was worth the vote. Well, wouldn't you know he never got those phones to his ears? We talked the whole flight back to LA.

"This is kind of gross . . ." he said as the plane was landing. "I've never asked a girl for her number on a plane ride before, but how about if I give you mine and you can call me if you ever want to go out and have a cup of coffee sometime?"

"Neat," I said. And accepted the cutest guy in the airport's number.

Betsy the playwright was picking me up at the airport. I met her down in Baggage so she wouldn't have to park her car.

"How was the flight?" she asked.

"Great," I answered. "I met this really nice guy who gave me his number."

"Gross." She was disgusted.

"I know. I'll never call him, but he was nice."

"What was his name?" she asked as we put my bags in the back-seat of her Toyota.

"Lindsey something."

"Lindsey who?"

"I can't remember," I said. "He's a musician."

"A musician?"

"Yeah."

She paused and looked at me sideways as she slammed her door. "Is he famous?"

"I don't think so," I said. "Maybe, though."

She was getting frustrated. My lack of pop culture knowledge had gotten in the way of our communication before. "Was he sitting in first class?" she asked.

"Yeah. That's how we met. He was sitting next to me."

"Buckingham? Was his last name Buckingham?"

"Yeah! That's it." I said it all excited like she had won the quiz.

"Lindsey Buckingham just gave you his phone number? Do you have any idea who he is, Anne?"

"Obviously not, B."

"He's the fucking lead guitarist of Fleetwood Mac, Anne!" She said it like I was a little stupid.

"Well how the hell am I supposed to know who Fleetwood fucking Mac is?"

Betsy rolled her eyes as we pulled into the airport traffic. "You're calling him," she said. "If for no other reason except for me to meet him."

"You got it."

We drove for a minute.

"I can't believe you met Lindsey fucking Buckingham and didn't know who he was."

"I can't either." I wanted to agree.

"Was he cute?"

"He won my vote."

"Was he old?"

"Old? What's old?" I figured her definition and mine would be different.

"Does he have wrinkles?"

"No, no wrinkles."

Betsy and I were doing another play together that she wrote

about abortion. Clinton was up for election and we were dead set on doing anything in our power to get the Republicans out. It was a one-woman show and I was the woman. I figured it would be a great excuse to call Mr. No Wrinkles. I asked him to come to the show after I made sure he was a Democrat. Older men I could handle, but Republicans were out.

He brought me a CD before we went to the show and I was blown away. I was blown away, and then he was blown away. At least that's what he said. Men will say anything to get a girl into bed, I'm aware of that now. I wanted to believe him, and he may have told the truth, but that doesn't negate my notion of older men and their need for youth. I was on board with another guy in his forties/almost fifties who was trying to be in his twenties.

Lindsey and I traveled together for a while while he was on tour, and I tried to be the good girlfriend groupie. We had fun for about a year. We played, we sang. But I was playing for him and not for me. I needed my own career and wasn't willing to sacrifice it for a rock star. I had just gotten cast in a John Frankenheimer movie and it seemed like the perfect time to make the split. Good-bye, Lindsey. Hello, Nashville.

> *Don't stop thinkin' about tomorrow.*
> *Don't stop, it'll soon be here.*
> *It'll be better than before.*
> *Yesterday's gone. Yesterday's gone.*

CHAPTER ELEVEN

THE MONSTER AND ME

My last session with Arthur was worse than my first. Or better, I suppose, depending on how you look at it. It was worse when I was in it, and better when I was out. I went into the session with an open mind, willing to confront anything that I saw of myself, but I was not prepared to see what I saw or feel what I felt. I thought that if it got difficult, I could get help—that's what Arthur had told me. But once I was in, I was so far in that I couldn't ask for help, I couldn't ask for anything. It wasn't the image of myself that I saw that day, it was the image of my father. He was on top of me, just like I had seen fragments of before in Dr. Ernst's office. But this time it was real. The whole picture. I was confronting my monster. He was on top of me, burying my face in a pillow, pulling me onto all fours, and raping me.

When you are deep into a journey, you are the age, the strength, and the size that you were at the time of the memory. It feels exactly as if you are there and it is happening to you all over again. At first I went into the same mode as in Dr. Ernst's office where my entire body went limp. I tried to disappear into the pillow, make my body as detached from the experience as possible. When it didn't stop the monster, I started to scream. I screamed out for my mother to come and stop him. I screamed and screamed until I had no lung power left and my throat was raw. When I realized that my voice was gone and no one was going to come and save me, I began my fight. I was precise with my actions at first. I very carefully tried to maneuver my elbows to a place where I could wound him, but my arms were too tiny and frail to overcome his strength and weight. Next, I balled my hands into fists and started beating at him to get off of me, but again I was too weak. When I realized that my arms could not protect me, I mustered all the strength I could into my entire body and began a fight I would fight for the next eight hours. For eight straight hours I fought to get my monster off of me.

My fists and legs were flailing uncontrollably as the terror of my abuse overtook every part of my being. I became consumed with the rage of what I felt each time my monster raped me, and I was determined that he wasn't going to win this time. I was going to do anything to get him off and win the battle once and for all. Arthur had to hold my arms down to stop me from beating myself, but he allowed the fight and the struggle. He knew I had to win, he knew how difficult it had to be, he knew that I had to feel all of it to release it once and for all and *get the monster off*. The more he held me down, the harder I fought. I became exhausted, but I didn't care—my weakness was not going to hold me back. I found strength in places I didn't know I had. When one part of me stopped moving from exhaustion, another kicked into gear. As the day went on, my voice came back and I found the courage in my language to match the courage in my body.

"Get off me, you motherfucker! Get off me!"

When my voice joined the fight, there was no stopping me. I don't know how I did it, but I stopped believing in my monster and started believing in myself. He became weak and I became strong. I don't know where it came from. It was deep and guttural and as vicious and vile a fight as he had fought me with. But, this time, he was the loser.

"GET OFF ME! YOU THINK YOU CAN DO THIS TO ME, YOU MOTHERFUCKER? YOU THINK THIS IS OKAY? THIS IS NOT OKAY. YOU CANNOT DO THIS TO ME! I AM YOUR DAUGHTER AND THIS IS NOT OKAY YOU FUCKING PIECE OF SHIT. YOU NOTHING. YOU RAPIST. YOU HORRID, HORRID CREATURE. YOU ARE NOT MY FATHER. YOU DO NOT DESERVE ME. YOU ARE A FUCK-ING MONSTER. NOW GET THE FUCK OFF! GET. THE. FUCK. OFF. OF. ME. NOW!"

And he was gone. The strength I had found was not in my body. There is no way an infant, a three-year-old, a six-year-old, or even a twelve-year-old can fight a grown man. He had taken control of my body, but he didn't have control of my mind. I was alive. He was dead. I was strong. He was weak. I had me. He did not. I wasn't his to take anymore. I never was.

Abusers do not take away the soul, the mind, the heart, or even the body of their victims. Something terrible is done to us, something they can only do because we are smaller than they. But we are *not* weaker. *They* are the weak.

How pathetic that some people have to take out their self-hatred on innocent children less than half their own size. How horribly fucking pathetic. When we are young and vulnerable, we want to believe that adults know more than we do, that they exert their control because they know better. In many cases, that's true. In the case of my father and every single person who abuses a child, that is not true. Once we understand that who we are when we come into this world cannot be taken away by anyone, no matter what they do to us to make us believe otherwise, we can begin to embrace our-selves.

Working with Arthur gave me an understanding of myself that I believe I would not have achieved otherwise. I have not done LSD since.

CHAPTER TWELVE

HELLO, DADDY

I met Dillon back when I was hangin' with the cool crowd. He wasn't around all of the time because he was a little older, but boy was he ever cool. He reeked cool. He reeked hip. He had the clothes and the hair product. He had an openness and freshness to his face. A simple purity. But he also had a fucked-up background the other cools seemed to lack. As Kale had said so succinctly years before, kids with fucked-up childhoods get along great. And we did. I don't know how we started spending time together, but we started as friends. I had rented a condominium down by the beach to give myself a new perspective. I thought being by the ocean would clear my mind and allow me time away from the hustle of Hollywood to take walks with my dog and find inner peace.

I was right. Being so far away from everyone made it easy to isolate myself. I liked being alone and was kind of awkward around others anyway. I was very tender from my last session with Arthur. Dr. Mann and I were working on healing my wounds, but I was like a puppy, all gangly and floppy when I wasn't in public pretending to be fine. I still *always* pretended to be fine. This was a layer that would take many more years and a stint as a gay-rights activist to finally peel off me.

Dillon would come down to the beach and we would sit in front of the fire and talk for hours, sipping tea and watching the flames. We were comfortable together. We shared stories and revealed ourselves in a way I had never done. There was nothing hidden between Dillon and me; I guess because we started as friends, we had no expectation that we had to be anything to each other besides supportive. We gave easily of ourselves and without judgment. I began missing him when he wasn't around. I felt safer when he was. I loved looking at his face, in his eyes. I liked his tales and family stories. Him. I liked him.

I got a movie that was going to take me to Cincinnati that I nicknamed *Milk Duds* upon arrival. I was trying out my hookering skills on-screen, what a treat! What a stretch as an actress! But sometimes you have to pay the rent, and I liked Melanie Griffith and Ed Harris, who were the stars.

Dillon and I were in the beginning stage of love. We hadn't had sex, and didn't want to force anything. He was cautious and careful with me, knowing what he knew, and he wanted me to feel comfortable about sex before we had it. He took me to the airport and through tears we said good-bye. Before I got on the plane he handed me a present and told me he wouldn't stop thinking about me and would visit if he could.

Annie Cincinnati [he had given me a nickname]—I want you to know that I love you. I care for you, your body and . . . the sex we'll someday have.

His present was a *Kama Sutra*–esque book called *The Art of Sexual Healing.* Amazing. The book talked about healing the sexual wounds in your body that are stored in your erogenous zones and how your lover can help heal you through lovemaking. Well, shit! I was beside myself. I was in love. Every night we talked on the phone. I would read him passages from the book and tell him how wonderful he was, and he would tell me about his day and how wonderful I was. And then we just couldn't stand it any longer—he had to fly to see me so that we could have sex.

I felt like I was preparing for my first love to get off the plane. It was almost like I had been re-virginized in the time that we had spent getting to know each other. It had been enough time that my body was able to stabilize and relax into itself. I bought flowers and candles and anything I could to make my little hotel room apartment look cozy and sensual for his arrival. But I don't think he saw any of it. From the time he walked through the door we were too enmeshed in each other's arms, kissing and holding and staring in the other's eyes, to see what the room had to offer. We were consumed in our love. We were ready for our love.

Making love with Dillon was different from any sexual love I had had. It was passionate, it was easy, it was enjoyable. I guess that was the biggest difference: I enjoyed it. I enjoyed everything about it. And wouldn't you know it, I had an orgasm? My first one. God bless Dillon; I hope he's not embarrassed if he's reading this. He changed my life forever. And for the better!

We had two years together that were fairly blissful as I remember. I was growing up and he was growing up. My career was on a steady rise and we tried to balance my time away with visits that kept us connected. But I still had some holes from wounds yet unhealed that Dillon couldn't fill. I wasn't conscious of them even as I started pulling away. That's the problem with holes, you think someone other than you can fill them, and when they can't you look for someone else to do it. I was looking, but I didn't know what for until I saw him falling out of the sky.

. . .

I was hired to play the "bad girl" in a small-town story of a man who finds a baby girl in the snow outside his house. The man takes her into his house and cares for her. After not being able to find the parents, he adopts the baby as his own. It was called *A Simple Twist of Fate,* and boy was it ever.

My first vision of Steve was of him sailing down from the sky in a multicolored hot-air balloon holding a girl about four years old in his arms. It was the most beautiful image: a man and his daughter floating to the ground in an embrace that would have crowds dabbing tissues at their eyes. Before the balloon landed and the director yelled *cut!* I already had a notion of this man, this Steve Martin guy I had barely heard of, implanted in my heart. He was magical, I thought. What guy who wasn't magic would write such a beautiful story about the love of a daughter? He didn't even have a daughter. Why couldn't my father have been like him? I thought.

When Steve climbed out of the basket, he was told I was on the set and came walking toward me with a big smile on his face. He was cuter than I imagined he would be. I had only seen one movie of his, and couldn't really remember what he looked like from it, but somewhere in my head I had determined that comedians couldn't be cute. Boy was I wrong. (Where do ideas like that come from in you, Anne? Comedians are cute, of course they're cute. Look at Steve. Steve is cute!)

"Hi, Steve!" I said in a tone that wouldn't give away what I was thinking.

"Hi, Anne!" He had a good voice. Deep, mellow. Mellow like yellow, and I liked yellow. He might have even been wearing yellow. He was sunny and bright. He was light. Like a Lite-Brite. All of a sudden everything in my head was childlike and good, and I was projecting it all onto his face.

"That was gorgeous."

"Isn't that fun? I've always wanted to ride in a hot-air balloon."

"Today was your day!"

"Today was my day," he agreed.

"I'm so glad I got to see it. Are you going to do it again?"

"No, I think we got it. We did a couple of shots before you got here."

"Well, lucky me, then. I would have hated to miss it. Was it as fun as you thought it would be?"

"Funner."

"Really?"

"Really. Sometimes I put scenes in movies just so I can do things that I've always wanted to do. This was one of those things."

"And it was funner than you thought," I said.

"Funner," he said.

"I like that word, 'funner.' "

"I like it too. Funner."

"Funner." We said *funner* back and forth and it was clear that the first Steve meeting was funner than I had thought it would be. "You're funner than I thought you would be. Comedians have a bad reputation," I joked.

"The un-fun kind of reputation?"

"Yep," I smiled.

"Everything you hear is bullshit. Haven't you learned that yet?"

I had heard that before, and I was beginning to believe it. Maybe the whole rap I had given men who were forty/almost fifty was bullshit too. Maybe I should rewrap my own rap.

"Hey, a couple of us are going out to a great diner in town tonight. You want to join us?" That sounded nifty.

"Well, that sounds nifty, Steve. I'd love to."

The nifty guy from the sky planned to pick me up at my hotel because he had a car and I didn't know where I was going. At least that was his excuse, and I bought it. The jury was still out on the whole rap on men business, but it didn't matter, I told myself. Steve and I weren't going to date or anything. Not even close. No way, nohow!

We drove to the diner in Atlanta in Steve's rent-a-car, which looked a lot like the sedan that I used to be driven in to work in my soap days. I liked being driven around by Steve. I liked Steve.

There was only one other person from the movie waiting in a corner booth when we arrived. Steve kind of put his head down and placed a cap so as not to draw attention to himself, but everyone turned their heads anyway.

"I hope you don't mind I brought company. Anne, this is Gabriel, Gabriel, Anne."

"Nice to meet you, Gabriel. I didn't mean to interrupt your dinner. I thought a lot of people were going to be here from the cast." I said it kind of pointedly so that Steve would know I wasn't an imbecile.

"Not at all," Gabriel said. "We're just two boring old guys moaning about their divorces. We could use the distraction."

We scooted into the booth, and I obviously wasn't a distraction enough, because all night long I heard tales of woe about women and divorce. Suddenly the light wasn't so bright. The magic not so magical. There was real pain in this man. And I knew pain. I was comfortable with pain. More comfortable with pain than pleasure. He needed taking care of, comforting. I was good at that. I felt right at home with Steve.

· · ·

Dillon invited me to spend Christmas with his family because he knew that I didn't go home for Christmas anymore. My last Christmas had been so bad that I made a vow to myself to quit family Christmases altogether. Holidays in general with my family were a nightmare. We didn't know how to communicate with one another at all. We had all gone completely different directions in our lives and didn't understand the others one bit. Abi hated Susan, Susan hated us both, and I roamed somewhere in the middle of it all, confused and outraged at them. The cycle changed sometimes, but generally there was a lot of hate going around. We knew nothing about each other. They knew nothing of my abuse, and certainly they had never said that they had been abused; we just simply didn't connect. We each thought that what the others were doing to keep their lives together was wrong. Everyone wanted everyone else to be doing it her way. Abi was stripping, Susan was popping out kids and having an affair, I was taking drugs and playing hookers, and my mother stayed blinded to it all while buried in her Bible. We couldn't tell the truth about anything that we felt, so we pretended we liked one another when we were together, just as we had pretended our whole lives. We shoved our truths into their respective pockets, plastered smiles on our faces, and talked about nothing. It's sad, because now that we've all changed our "bad behaviors," we've stopped communicating altogether. I guess it's more truthful than pretending, but it's still a heartbreak.

The last Thanksgiving I attended, Jud killed a deer in their backyard and brought it in, proud of his slaughter.

"Venison? Anyone for venison?" Jud gave me the creeps. He always did. I knew that Susan was cheating on him, but I pretended like I didn't when I saw him.

"Venison! Wow, you're a hunter?"

Susan judged me for having sex out of wedlock, but she pretended that she didn't when she saw me.

"Have you ever hunted before, Anne? Abi? Anyone hunt?"

I wondered about the children and the family relationships they would have.

Do you kids like to hunt too? Do you play with guns? Rifles? Any of you kill anything yet?

We were watching our family lie being re-created in front of our eyes, but we pretended that we weren't. Each time Susan got pregnant, my mother would call me on the phone like the Second Coming was coming.

I love my nieces and nephews. They are extraordinary kids from what I know of them, but I hate to admit that's not much. Susan and I stopped speaking after she walked out on me in a restaurant one night in New York when I told her I had an idea for a story I was going to call *Stripping for Jesus,* about my perspective on my childhood. She was horribly offended that I would write anything with such a title and got up from the dinner table when Jud was in the bathroom. Jesus apparently was off limits as subject matter, and stripping was more than she could handle. The combination was vile and I was the root of all evil, according to her. When Jud came back, Susan was gone, and all he could offer up as an excuse for her behavior was that "she does this sometimes."

And then he bolted to join her. I didn't speak to them again until my mother called me and begged me, for her sake, to try it with Susan one more time. She hated that her daughters didn't get along. She and her sister had fought all of their lives, and she didn't want the same fate for us. It was Christmas after all, and Christmas was a time for giving gifts.

"She walked out on me, Mother. *She* walked out on *me*. Shouldn't you be having this conversation with her?"

"I know, Anne, but you're the bigger of the two of you. I know you're younger, but you're going to therapy and have done so much work on yourself. Couldn't you please try this one more time, for me? Please, Anne?"

My mother didn't yet know of all the work I was doing. She knew that I was in therapy, but she didn't know what for. I wanted my mother to love me. I thought that if I did this one thing for her, maybe I would connect with her enough to be able to tell her what really happened to me.

So I did it. I flew myself to Chicago and rented a car with my mother and drove out to the wealthy suburb where Susan and Jud lived, to try to make peace with my sister. We got out of the car and trudged through the billowing snow to get to their front door.

Their house was not dissimilar to the century home we had lived in so many years before. It was old and white and had black shutters, and from inside I could hear the piano playing like I had so often before when my father would play. As Mom creaked open the door, I could immediately smell the Christmas tree and burning fire. The smell wafted in strange harmony with the chords of the song Susan was playing: "My Favorite Things," from *The Sound of Music*. I used to sing that song with my father, and I thought Susan was playing it for me as an apology. She was a jazz pianist and the chords were discordant and eerie. The innocent melody was gone, and it seemed appropriate, truthful. She didn't make eye contact as I walked over to the piano and settled behind her. I figured words were hard for her to muster, so I tried in my own way to say I forgave her.

"Finally," I said with sad understanding, "the way it should have always been played in our house."

Without any reply, she briskly lifted her hands off of the keys and stomped out of the room and up her old staircase, as if she'd never come down again.

I looked at Jud, who was standing there as shocked as my mother and I were. "She just does this sometimes, is that it, Jud?"

I grabbed my mother's arm and ran out of their house into the freezing cold, where I could speak away from earshot of the children. "How dare you. How dare you make me come here and go through that." I was ashamed and hurt and too angry to cry.

"She didn't know I was coming, did she? Did she? You didn't have the guts to tell her that *she* hurt me and that *she* was responsible, that *she* should be apologizing to *me*. She walked out on me months ago and then she did it again!"

"I know, Anne, sweetheart. I know."

"You know what? That I'm a fucking asshole for listening to you? For flying here? For walking through that front door? For walking over to the piano? For being a complete fucking idiot? Is that what you know? You know that, Mom?"

"You're not an idiot. You tried."

"I *tried*? That's all you can say to me? You didn't even tell her I was coming! You didn't confront her at all, did you? You wanted *me* to put my feelings aside to make it all okay for *you* just like I always have, didn't you? Didn't you?"

My mother was crying her weepy cry that she cried when she felt guilty and wanted someone to take care of her. I had lived with her for seventeen years, and I knew what it was, what it sounded like, and it was making me sick to my stomach.

"Forgive me, Anne? Forgive me?" She was begging. I hated begging.

"This isn't about your feelings right now, Mother. You fucked me over. I flew myself here for you. I rented a fucking car for this—for this what? For this fucking treatment? For this nightmare? You told me that she knew I was coming. That we were going to work things out *together*! You lied to me. You fucking lied to me!"

"I'll never do it again, I promise. I'll never ask you to do anything like that again. I promise. Forgive me, please. I don't know what's wrong with your sister. I just don't know."

It was all too much. I got in the car seething and could barely stay in the driveway long enough for my mother to get in the car. I wanted to run her over. She would beg and plead and whine all the way back to Chicago about how it wasn't her fault and how my sister needed a lot of help.

YOU NEED HELP! I wanted to scream. YOU NEED HELP, MOTHER!!!!

Needless to say, that was the last Christmas I spent with my family, and I happily accepted Dillon's offer to be with his. He was a child of divorce, but his mother had remarried and they had two wonderful daughters whom Dillon bragged about and loved and couldn't wait to see. How refreshing, I thought. A family that wants to be together.

I flew to New York to join the festivities with the sadness of my family crudding my insides. I watched as Dillon and his family laughed and joked and shared stories and love for one another. I couldn't help but feel like an outsider in their celebration. "I'll never belong here," I thought. "It's too happy for someone like me."

After the presents were opened, Dillon took me on a walk through the snow up to the most beautiful peak in the most beautiful town outside of Manhattan. My insides started spilling out of my mouth in an unconscious rant that would leave us both devastated and alone by the end of the day. *Christmas is a time for giving,* I heard my mother say.

"I love you, you know that, right?" We were looking up at the sky, snow in our boots, but still warm from the fire.

"That's sweet," Dillon said. "You know I love you too?"

"Yeah. I do know that." I did know that. We walked a while longer and found another perch. "But we're so young," I continued.

"Yeah . . . ? We're young . . . ?"

I was twenty-four, he twenty-eight. "And it's not like this is going to last forever."

"What do you mean, forever?"

"Well, we've been dating for a while now and I'm having a really great time and all, but it's not like we're going to get married or anything." How could this convoluted train of thought *not* confuse him?

"What are you talking about, Anne?"

"Well, you love me and I love you, but we're so young, right? I mean . . . you can't tell me right now that you don't ever want to be with another girl in your whole life. I mean, can you?" Could he? Would he? I wanted to know. I needed to know.

"I don't know. I haven't thought about it like that," he said.

"Well, think about it now. Do you think that you'll never want to be with another girl? Can you say that for sure, right now to my face, you *never* want to be with anyone else ever again in your whole life?" I was desperate for the answer, pleading.

"Are you asking if I'm ready to get married?"

"Yeah. I guess I am. Are you willing to get married to me right now, or do you have reservations?"

"Well, if you put it that way, I guess I do."

I knew it. "Because you don't know and can't say that you don't want to be with anyone else, right? Otherwise you'd be willing to get married."

"Are *you* willing to get married to *me*?"

"I'm asking you, Dillon! Do you want to get married to me right now or not?"

"I don't think I'm ready to get married, no, but—"

"No buts. You see what I'm saying? If we're not willing to get married, then what are we waiting for?"

"What are we waiting for about what?"

"What are we waiting for to break up? If it's going to happen eventually, then why doesn't it happen now? It's *going* to happen, that's what you're saying—so I think we should do it now."

"Are you saying you want to break up?"

"You're not willing to say that you don't want to be with anyone else, so, yes, I guess I am." I was hurting and frustrated and my hurt was hurting him.

"I don't understand where this is coming from, Anne. I thought things were going really great between us."

"They are! But why postpone what's going to happen, if we know it's going to happen anyway?" My logic was so mature.

"You want to see other people? *Is that what you're telling me?*" Now he was getting angry. Our words were melting the snow and freezing our hearts.

"I'm just saying that if we think we're going to see other people eventually, then we should do it now. What are we waiting for?"

"Nothing, I guess. When you put it that way—we're waiting for nothing!"

"Exactly my point. I knew you didn't want to get married! I hope you like her, whoever she is."

My inability to communicate about my gaping holes had created a chasm between us that Dillon didn't know how to cross. I was shaking and frozen and terrified that I had made this Christmas end like all the others, but I didn't know how to stop myself. I wasn't comfortable with goodness and uncomplicated love yet. Looking back, I guess I didn't think I deserved it.

When the dog bites,
When the bee stings,
When I'm feeling sad,

I simply remember my favorite things,
And then I don't feel so bad.

I returned to Atlanta, where I still had a couple of weeks to shoot on Steve's movie. We started spending more time together. Each night we would have dinner and tell our tales of woe. I told him about my breakup with Dillon and he talked about his breakup with his wife. Consciously or unconsciously we were opening the door for the other to come in.

You can see the patterns; you know the ugly of me by now. The twist and contort game was about to start, and it was going to be disguised as love and even be love for a while. I don't want to diminish my time with Steve or even the feelings we had for each other, but onto the game board we crawled, full-bodied and ready to play. As if in an adult game of Twister, we got on all fours and began spinning the dial.

• • •

I left Steve in Atlanta to finish his movie and returned to my condo in LA to resume my work of auditioning and therapy. He wrote me love notes and letters unlike anything I had read. His mind was brilliant and expressive, our conversations filled with laughter and complexity. I fell in love with his mind. I didn't know much of his work and he preferred it that way, allowing our relationship to be built on the present of our interaction. I wanted to hear everything he had to say. He lived such a life, had learned so much, and had an amazing wisdom. I trusted his advice and comfortably shared my experiences with him.

I'd like to think that I was more than just a connection to youth for Steve. I really think we admired each other. But it was difficult. He was famous, I wasn't. He was wealthy, I was struggling. He was older, I was younger. We knew that people would have some judgment about these things, so we hid behind the walls of his house for the first six months we were together in order not to have to confront it.

Spin. Twist. Spin. Twist.

I pretended that it was okay. I had other things that were more important to me than being able to go out in public, I told myself. Steve knew about my past and encouraged me to write about it. I was nervous about writing; I had done very little, but I had a lot of ideas. I would need help. Steve offered. In fact, he insisted. He literally sat me down in front of a computer one day and taught me how to type in the first lines of an idea I had for a screenplay.

"Type: I-N-T period. A-P-A-R-T-M-E-N-T slash D-A-Y."

He stood over me as I learned how to type. He was patient with me as I learned the basics of writing a screenplay. He read every page with me as it shot out of the printer.

I attacked my writing like I had my acting. I was diligent about my work and exhilarated by the process. It wasn't only a hobby, but a way for me to express my inner thoughts, no matter how twisted they might be, in a form for others to read and perhaps someday perform. Directing was always in the forefront of my mind. I had five more years to reach my goal and a lot more to learn. I knew that to build a career you had to start from the bottom, and that's what I did. I wrote and directed a play with a friend in between movie shoots called *If I Fall,* a story about a girl and her abusive father. We nicknamed it *If I Fail* because we thought it might suck, but we put it up in a forty-nine-seat theater anyway. It did suck, but I was only just beginning. Next I wrote a screenplay called *The In-Betweens.* In the opening scene a six-year-old girl sees her father on the ground, lifeless. She kicks him in the head to see if he's dead. My manager at the time was appalled.

"Does she have to *kick* him in the head, Anne? Can't she just nudge him with her toe or something?"

"No, Nick, she can't *nudge* him with her toe," I argued. "It doesn't mean anything if she *nudges* him. She *has* to kick him. Don't you get it? It sets up her entire character!"

It would never get made but I didn't care. I was learning, I told myself. I started another script immediately. *Stripping for Jesus:* I typed the words on the title page. I holed up in Steve's office again and started tapping away.

Twist. Spin. Twist. Spin.

My contortions were subtle, and I told myself they didn't matter. I had a lot to learn from Steve. Just shut up and take it all in. I knew nothing about art, and Steve had one of the greatest collections from Hollywood to New York City. He taught me about each piece, each artist. He expanded my mind and taught me about culture. He played music for me and took me to the theater. I couldn't do these things for him. What could I teach him that he didn't already know?

Twist. Spin. Twist. Spin.

The first time Steve and I were going to show our faces in public together was for an event at MOCA honoring Roy Lichtenstein. When he bought me a conservative-looking dress for the museum occasion and every occasion after that, I swallowed the reality that I was dressing as someone other than myself. I told myself that I was looking respectable for his friends, for his public. I thought I was doing what he wanted me to do. I thought I was being a good girlfriend.

Twist. Spin. Twist. Spin.

I told myself that the age difference didn't matter to me. We told each other the same thing. We didn't want to be a cliché. We wanted to be a normal loving couple with normal loving needs. I didn't want to be seen as youthful arm candy, he didn't want to be seen as my father. When you're in a relationship with obvious differences, you'll tell yourself anything to cover your discomfort. You'll agree to the lie until the lie reveals itself to you and you are forced to face the truth.

Twist. Spin. Twist. Spin.

We hadn't moved in together and it had been almost two years of serious dating. Steve wanted to move from the house where he had lived with his ex-wife for ten years, and without much thought, we started looking. Neither broached the subject as we traveled down hallways and inspected each room.

"Look at this! This would be a great office for you."

"Nice closets, huh? I love a big closet."

"Can you believe the bathroom? So big, so nice."

"Really nice. I *did* see it and I liked what I saw."

I saw this and he saw that and we talked about absolutely nothing that really needed to be seen.

"This is the house," I said after our final tour.

"This is the house?" He needed to be sure.

"I've never seen such a dream."

"Your dream house, huh?"

"This is the house, Steve. This is the house."

When Steve made an offer on the house that was a dream, out came the pain of what we'd not foreseen. I was not willing to move in with Steve. When we looked for houses together, he had assumed I was ready to take that boundary away, but I wasn't. The reality that our relationship was not going to move forward crushed us both. I didn't want to be Mrs. Steve Martin. He hadn't asked, but where else was it going to go? He was a man now in his fifties; I was a girl in the middle of my twenties. I called my mother to tell her about the breakup and how sad I was.

"Steve must be devastated," she said. "Do you think he would be willing to go out with me? I always thought he liked me."

FRESNO, 2000

"Hello? Hello? Is anybody there? Hello?"

I was standing in the backyard of a tiny farmhouse, in the middle of a dirt field. In fact, there were dirt fields surrounding the house. Dirt as far as the eye could see. I had been walking for about an hour, maybe two, in the dirt and my feet were extraordinarily dirty—not to mention my white cotton pants. I was also parched. You see, it was very hot as I said before, maybe upwards of a hundred and five by now. I thought I would keep walking in the dirt to my spaceship, but the ship was nowhere in sight. Only the little house.

I took everything as a sign, as I had the whole day, and I figured

I was getting another message that my time here on earth wasn't quite over. I needed perhaps to make just one more stop.

"Hello?" I called out again. There was a screen door off to the side of the house and a small patch of grass that was being rained on by a tiny plastic sprinkler. The patch was all of about ten feet by ten feet and I thought it wouldn't mind if I sipped some of its lubrication. Water had never tasted so good. I had forgotten to buy any water at the gas station. Or maybe not forgotten as much as I thought it wasn't necessary, seeing that I would be boarding soon and thought for sure the ship would be stocked with anything my heart or mouth desired.

"Yeah?"

I was startled by the young man's voice even though I had called out, and I turned around with a jump. He kind of jumped too. We were a jumpy twosome.

"Don't be alarmed," I said to the youngster. "I'm not going to hurt you."

The boy was dark-skinned and had big brown, searching eyes. I didn't think he had probably expected to see a sweaty white girl with her shirt off in his backyard that day. I didn't think he probably expected anyone in his backyard any day. It didn't look like anyone ever came around at all. Things were rusted and leaning on the side of the house, like a bike, a watering can, and some broken toys.

"I've been walking quite a ways and I'm absolutely parched. Would you mind giving me a glass of water?"

He motioned me to come inside as he propped open the door with his body.

"Thank you," I said. "Thank you ever so much."

I walked past him into a small kitchen littered with breakfast dishes and last night's dinner. There was a small table with some beer bottles on it and a young girl of about twelve standing at its side.

"Hello," I said.

"Hello," she said. She was very beautiful and had her long dark hair pulled back in a ponytail to keep her neck from the heat. She had a slight accent when she spoke.

"He doesn't speak much English," she explained.

"Oh, that's okay. I didn't mean to scare him, though. Was he scared?"

The boy was in the room, standing next to his sister, by this time. He shook his head adamantly.

"No," she said. "He's not scared."

"Good," I said. "Would it be too much trouble to have a glass of water?"

The girl didn't think that would be a problem and motioned for the boy to get it for me.

"Thank you. Thank you so much." I drank the glass in one gulp and wiped my lips. "I guess you're wondering what I'm doing standing in your kitchen half-dressed in my bra like this. I didn't expect to see anybody, and with the heat, I thought it would be more comfortable to walk without my shirt. I'm sorry for my appearance."

"That's okay. It's hot," she said. We stood there for a while not saying anything. I was waiting for my next message. I didn't quite know what I was doing there, and neither did they. We were an ignorant threesome. And then it came to me.

"Do you by any chance have a piece of paper and pencil or pen that I could borrow? I left my car way back on the road and I need to let people know where it is so they can find it once I'm gone."

As she got me the paper and pen she asked, "Where are you going?"

"To heaven," I said matter-of-factly. "My spaceship is going to land out here somewhere. I figure just outside the window. That field over there, I think." I pointed through the torn flowered curtains to the field I had walked across to get to the house.

"Heaven?" she asked.

"Heaven," I said. "You wanna come?"

She looked at her brother and he at her.

"I can take anybody I want. The ship is big enough for everybody. Everybody in the whole world."

"But why are you going to heaven?" It was a smart enough question.

"Because I want to live in a world of love. I've tried it here for too long and now I'm ready to go home. In heaven there is only love. There is no hardship and no pain and no war and no poverty." No poverty sounded appealing, I could tell.

"Heaven, like in the sky?" she asked.

"Like in the sky," I confirmed. "You wanna come? The ship will be here in about an hour."

She and her brother confirmed that they would like to come to a place of love and peace.

"But I need to take a shower first. Do you mind if I use your shower?" I was feeling faint and perhaps had a little sunstroke from the walk.

"You are a bit dirty," she said.

"Yes," I agreed. And she led me toward the washroom.

"I'm glad you're coming," I said. "There's going to be quite a celebration when we arrive."

• • •

I was sitting in Dr. Mann's office for my usual afternoon session and was fidgety and frustrated and angry and pissed.

"What is the matter with her?" I wanted Dr. Mann to tell me.

"I have no idea, Anne. Absolutely no idea."

"Well, at least you're honest. I mean, have you ever heard of such a thing? A mother asking her daughter if she can go out with her ex-boyfriend?"

"There have been stranger things that have happened to you, but this is certainly up there in the strange category."

"I mean, what the fuck is her problem? I called her to tell her about *me* and all she cares about is *him*. 'I'm sure he's devastated.' *I'm devastated!* I loved Steve. I mean, who the fuck knows? I loved him. He was my father . . . love . . . father . . . love . . . father . . . I don't know. I loved him even if he was a father figure; is that so wrong? I mean, shit! He was a great guy. I didn't want to marry him, but it doesn't mean my mother can have him. And he loved me! He doesn't want to marry my mother! He doesn't want to *fuck* my mother! He did not fall in love with my last fucking name!"

"It's absurd. I agree with you."

"He gave her a pair of glasses one time. A pair of reading glasses. That's why she thinks he liked her, because she liked his reading glasses and then he bought her a pair to be nice and sent them to her. To be nice—*not* because he wanted to *fuck* her. Jesus! What is the matter with my family?"

Dr. Mann looked at me like—Duh.

"I know. Duh. It's too much. But she's fucking crazy."

"She may be, but what's important is that she's driving you crazy. You need to confront her about *your* feelings when you're having them and not keep them inside because you're afraid to hurt *her* feelings. You don't need to take care of her, Anne. You need to take care of you."

I sat with the information for a long while. Then I asked a question I had been waiting to ask for two years. "You think I should tell her?" I was direct and wanted a direct response.

"I can't make that decision for you, Anne. Do you feel ready to tell her?" That was not as direct as I wanted.

"I don't know. I mean, I guess I am. Why not? If I don't tell her now, I don't know when I'm going to tell her. It's not like there's going to be a day when it'll be like *Hey! What a great day to tell my mother that my father fucked me! I sure hope she's home!*"

"That day probably won't happen, no."

"Christ. This sucks." I sat there feeling it suck for a while. My leg was twitching, a habit I had acquired in Dr. Mann's office when a lot of emotion was coming up. "I have to tell her."

"Okay."

"I'm gonna call her when I get home."

"Are you sure you're ready?"

"I'm ready as I'll ever be."

I left Dr. Mann's office before my time was up and went home to call my mother and tell her about my abuse for the first time in my life. I was twenty-six years old. After a long and brutal conversation my mother hung up the phone on me.

Jesus loves you Anne . . . Jesus loves you Anne . . . Jesus loves you Anne Jesus loves you Anne Jesus you Anne Jesus loves you Anne Jesus you AnneJesus loves youAnneJesus lovesAnneJesusyou you AnneJesus- youAnneJesus lovesAnneJesusAnneJesus AnneJesusAnneJesusAnne- JesusAnneJesusAnneJesus . . .

PART THREE

•

BECOMING JESUS

CHAPTER THIRTEEN

TWELVE DAYS

The best thing about going crazy is you never know when it's going to happen, so you can't prepare yourself or be scared of it. You can be casually walking down the street one day and WHAMMO! it happens, just like that—you're on the ground on all fours, straddling the curb of a Manhattan sidewalk in front of Ray's pizza parlor. You don't know what hit you. You look around for some sort of explanation, a bicyclist picking up their bike, a man gathering his briefcase, a woman dusting herself off—but there is nothing. There's only you, the curb, and a very strong premonition that God is talking to you. That's right—God is talking to you. You don't know if anyone else is hearing it, but from the continuous hustle and bustle, you gather that no one else is. You try to collect your legs from under your body and pretend you didn't just fall facefirst onto the ground.

"Hello? Hello?" you might call out while checking for broken bones. "God, what the fuck was that?"

And like nothing you've ever imagined, God answers back. "Yes, Anne?"

"What?"

"You asked, 'What the fuck?'"

"God? Is that you?"

"Yes, it is true."

You search the skies for loudspeakers and see none. "Jesus, I must be crazy."

"No, but you *are* Jesus."

Now you get even more concerned about your mental health than the moment before. "Oh, God!"

"That's right. Jesus, God, Anne. That's what you are, Anne. Jesus. God."

"You've got to be kidding me. Is this some kind of joke?"

"No joke, Anne. You are God."

"Holy shit."

"Holy, yes. Shit, no."

I had seen crazy people talking to the sky and surrounding area before, and now I was one of them. It concerned me a great deal. I tried to cover my mouth and collect my thoughts, but there was no collecting to be done. The more I collected, the more I heard God.

"I don't understand what's happening right now, so if I could have a little break, that'd be great, God."

"No breaks anymore, Anne. Didn't you think there was a reason, a purpose to all the work that you've done?"

"Yeah, so shit like this wouldn't happen to me."

"You wanted to be healed, find love. Well, you have. You're healed. You are love. Pure and simple and sent from above."

"You're telling me that I'm from heaven?"

"That's right."

"Sent from above to find love?"

"That's right. And you have. You are it. You are love. And now you must teach it to all who want to hear."

"This whole conversation is sounding a bit crazy, I'll have you know, God. I don't want to be rude or anything like that because, after all, you are God, but this is fucking whacked." I was now walking toward no particular destination, but I thought if I walked, God would go away and find a gutter somewhere.

"You can't get away from me, Anne. You are my daughter. I know you have felt like I have not been there for you, but you needed to find love in yourself before you could know who you are."

I suddenly began floating about an inch off the ground. "What's this? Some kind of goddamn trick?"

"No trick, Anne. Just you."

"I don't get it. Who am I?"

I stayed floating, but kept walking. I figured if it looked like I was walking, no one would notice that I wasn't touching the ground.

"You are God. God in the flesh. I am God in spirit."

"And you're telling me that I am your daughter?"

"That's right."

"Like Jesus was your son."

"That's right."

"I am the Second Coming?"

"You are the Second Coming."

"But what about Jesus? I thought he was coming back."

"It wouldn't be very fair to have me be a male both times on earth, would it?"

"Why not? Isn't that what the Bible says?"

"The Bible was written by men."

"So it's prejudiced?"

"Very."

"I've always wondered about that."

"I know."

"But I didn't come from a virgin."

"Neither did he."

I always knew the Bible was full of it. "That's really gonna piss some people off."

"People believe what they want to believe," God said.

"You can say that again," I said.

"People believe what they want to believe," God said again.

"Thanks, God."

"You're welcome."

I thought God was quite clever and enjoyable to talk with. I decided to walk with him for a while. "So where is Jesus from?"

"Heaven."

"Oh, I get it."

"Do you?"

"Yeah, he's not from Mary, he's from heaven."

"Right. Just like you."

"I'm not from my mother either."

"Exactly."

"I'm from heaven."

"You're beginning to get it now, Anne."

God and I walked all day like that. Then we walked all night. He told me we were going to be together for twelve days straight. God needed me to know who I was. I had a lot to learn about being Jesus, and he was going to be my teacher.

• • •

It's very difficult to describe the next twelve days of my life to you, because I still don't know exactly how or why it happened to me. I only have my theories, which I will share. I am not a doctor and I have not consulted a therapist about my explanations. It's important for you to know that there were no drugs involved. I had stopped LSD therapy three years prior to this occurrence. I was actually feeling more grounded in my life than I had for years, other than the issues with my mother. The phone call with her happened less than three weeks before my first encounter with God on the street.

I believe that my mother's reaction to my abuse was too painful for me to absorb and sent me to a place in my subconscious that seemingly negated my need for her love. I believe that my mind created a false reality that directly connected me with God. I believe that I connected with God because of my religious teachings about him as a child. By receiving the love of God, I no longer focused on what I was lacking in my family. I was, as God told me, *pure love sent from above to teach love.* In this reality there was no room for me to feel sorrow about my past or the pain of my family's reaction in the present. I determined that the very purpose for being born into my abusive environment was so I could have compassion and understanding for others who had experienced similar things as children. I developed theories to relieve my parents of any responsibility for the pains they caused me. If God wanted me to experience life the way that I had, then I couldn't blame anything on my parents anymore. I could forgive them for all they had done and love them for the lessons they gave.

During these twelve days of my life I was at the complete mercy of my mind. My body and anything that it did were out of my control. It was the scariest, most invigorating, most insane-making period of my life. It is a time that affected my whole being for the next four years, until I could get a handle on what it was about and let it go. In my mind I became Jesus. I was called Celestia, the reincarnation of God. I believed that I was the Second Coming here to teach the world about pure love. I believed that each and every person on this planet was God, and I was here to show them their reflection. I believed that I was born to tell this truth to the world, just like Jesus believed he was. I believed I was given my calling by God in heaven. I believed that I was going to become famous to do this.

I had never wanted to be famous without something to say. Now, I thought, my work to become a successful actress had its purpose.

• • •

The first order of business was to get two leather-bound books to write down the messages I was receiving. This was to be my Bible, the new Bible of truth, and I was going to write it based on what God told me. I was led, and by led I mean told by God, to go into a specific store in downtown Manhattan to make the purchase. I had absolutely no idea where I was being told to go or what I was going to do there. I trusted in God completely and gave my body and mind over to him. I was also very aware that I was Anne Heche, an actress. I knew I was a person with friends and a life existing alongside the life I was now living as Celestia.

I walked everywhere. I was told when to turn, where to turn, and when to stop. When I was at the right place, I would hover and wait for my next instructions. My first stop was outside a leather shop in Greenwich Village. I had never been to or seen the shop before. I knew that I was supposed to be getting some books, but the leather shop only had belts, purses, and bags in the window. I told God that I thought we had come to the wrong place. Please note that God and I only spoke telepathically; I did not speak out loud, I did not draw attention to myself in any way. Although I always felt like I was floating and not walking, God promised me that no one would notice. I was always safe, God said. No one would know anything about what was going on with me until it was time. God told me to walk into the store.

When I looked inside, there were no books anywhere at all. I began to get anxious and fear that I had gone completely nuts. I didn't know how to stop the insanity in my head and begged for God to leave me alone.

"You don't by any chance have any leather books, do you?" I heard the words coming out of my mouth and into the ears of the clerk.

"Leather books . . . leather books . . ." He was searching his mind. I was fearing mine.

"You know, it's funny you should ask . . ."

"Oh? How so?"

He reached down behind the counter and into a drawer or hidden shelf. "I have two of them. They've been here forever. I didn't order any more 'cause they didn't sell. Could this be what you're looking for?" The man put two leather books on the counter in front of me. One was black and the other a deep green.

"They're exactly what I was looking for, thank you. I'll take them." When we were outside I had a thought that maybe this Jesus stuff was going to be funner than I thought.

"You can enjoy this, you know. Love is fun," God said. I didn't so much mind having someone read my mind.

"So . . . what's next?" There was a hint of enthusiasm in my head about my next adventure.

"Let's get some music," God said. "Turn left here."

I closed my eyes and floated down the aisles with my fingers touching the tops of all the CDs. I didn't want to be swayed in any way by my taste, hence, the shut-eye. When I arrived at a CD I was to purchase, my fingers would grab at the case and I would move on. When I got to the register I had twelve plastic packages in my hands.

"Quite a selection you've got here." My CDs were put in a bag and I was off. I had no idea what I had bought.

I spilled the contents of the bag onto my friend's couch. Lisa Light—Light, I called her—was a friend I had met in New York while I was shooting *The Juror* and *Walking and Talking*. We had had an immediate connection when we met and she and her boyfriend and I all became great friends. Whenever I was in the city I would call them and we would spend most of my free time together. Michael, her beau, wasn't home when I arrived on their front stoop. God thought we needed privacy for the first of many conversations about what was happening to me. Light became my confidante and so much more. As we perused the contents of the small packages I told her what had happened to me, from start to finish.

"I've always known this about you, Anne," Light said when I had finished.

"What? What do you mean?"

"Since I was a girl I've been having a dream about a blond-haired woman who was going to come into my life. I was told that I was here to help her. She was going to have a very special purpose here on this planet. I have been waiting for you to know. I have known since the first time we met."

We had known each other now for about three years, and she had never mentioned a word. We had had many conversations about God and religion and belief. She was Jewish and her faith in God was strong.

"So you don't think I'm crazy?"

"I don't think you're crazy at all. I will help you write the books."

"And what about the CDs?" I asked. "Why these?"

"They tell the old story," she said. "You are here to tell the new one." On every one of the CDs was some sort of religious iconography, some depiction of Jesus or Mary. There was a different selection from each type of music in the store, all with the same theme. I was holding *Jesu, Joy of Man's Desiring* in my hand.

"This is unbelievable" was all I could think to say. I was exhausted and confused and scared.

"Take it slow, Celestia. You have eleven days ahead of you."

• • •

Days became nights and nights became days. There was no clear distinction of time. I had a lot to learn about being God, and I was determined to learn my lessons well. I had just finished shooting *Donnie Brasco,* which is why I was in New York. I was staying at the Shoreham Hotel on West Fifty-fifth Street and figured that I had been given a clean space with no distractions to learn my lessons. The room I was staying in had clean white walls, two beds, and a beautiful bathroom. There was a CD player in a cabinet I discovered only the night I returned from Light's. I was told to put on a CD, get a pen, and open the black leather book.

I wrongly assumed that I would be writing things that I could understand. We all know what happens when you assume. God had something else in store for me. A surprise, if you will. He had a whole language I had never heard or seen that poured out of my mind and into my hand. As soon as I took hold of the pen, my fingers began writing symbols, not letters. I had no control over what my pen was writing. When it started and stopped was not up to me.

I let the energy guide me. I knew that I was forming sentences and paragraphs of some sort because there were periods and page turns and indents, but other than that I had no idea what I was doing, if I would ever know, or if I would ever be able to figure it out. I think a few days passed in the hotel as I finished and filled the first leather book. When my Bible was completed, I could not understand one word of it. That would be the next adventure.

The book never left my body. I kept it in my backpack when I finally stepped outside to see the light of day. It was beautiful and sunny outside and smelled fresh and clean. I saw and felt everything in a new way. My attachment to the world that I lived in had deepened in my time writing. I hadn't known what I was actually putting on the page, but the idea of it had somehow washed through me.

God is love. The world is love. There is no pain unless we agree to pain. War is an ugly battle of ego. Ego must die. We are all God.

None of these concepts were foreign to me. I had heard them in churches and on radios. I had felt them in my own heart. But spending hours with God and only God had made me somewhat cleaner, clearer, and more appreciative of everything around me. As I began looking at each element of the city—the buildings, the street signs, the people, the homeless, the shops—I began seeing the details of what each thing was made of. The materials, the cloth, the fabric, the colors, the eyes, the skin, the hair . . . and it all became of equal importance in my mind. The smaller the detail, the more it all made sense to me. We are all one thing. Without one thing, we cannot have another.

As I took apart each thing to its barest minimum, I began hearing words for each of the things I was seeing. Words I had never heard before. A language was wafting through my ears. I took out my notebook and began writing. Cab = such and such. Traffic light = so and so. Person = this or that. I was teaching myself and being taught a new language. A language of love. Everything in this language was equal. There was no gender, no lesser than or greater than. I walked the streets for a couple of days, absorbing and writing down everything that I could until I was sure I had it.

The language of love also had a sound. I would pronounce each word as I learned it and feel it trickle over my tongue. It was lovely. It was sweet to say and hear. It was calm and almost like a song, with beats and rhythm. It was lighthearted and jovial. Pleasurable to the ear. I started to speak to God in this language. I would adopt this language as my own.

Messages were coming to me all the time now, and sometimes I couldn't write them down as fast as I heard them. I needed help. I decided to teach Light the language so that she could write while I spoke. We began our sessions together by talking and translating the book.

I was about halfway through my twelve-day period when Light showed up with a badly twisted ankle. She could barely walk because of the swelling and was in a lot of pain. She didn't know if we would be able to do the session. We settled her onto the couch in my room and propped up her foot.

"You can heal it," I heard her say. "Did you hear me?"

I was trying to ignore what I heard and grabbed for my pen and book.

"You can heal. You have the power. I know you do."

The language was one thing, but healing another. I was scared that we were entering some territory that was too Jesus-like. Was I supposed to think that I could do everything that Jesus did? Is this what she was trying to tell me?

"Yes, Anne," I heard God say. But the *yes* was now like a sound, more like a *qui* than a yes, but more like a musical note than a foreign sound. God also had another name. God was not "God" in our language. It was "Quiness." At least that's how we spelled it. It was the named representation of both the female and male in God. God as one, genderless God.

"Oh, Quiness. Nakka dune notta." Oh, my God. I cannot do this. "Ik all notra daska don." It's too scary for me now. I was talking aloud to God so that Light could hear me.

"Balla." That was the word for baby. "Ista forka dunna dol." It is your fortune to heal. "Sunka dorma." Let it be.

I cried at the thought of being able to heal another person. I had heard all of the stories from the Bible of Jesus and his powers, and certainly I thought it would be wonderful to be able to do such things. But even as the Second Coming herself, it seemed a bit lofty.

"Just try it," Light said. "The worst that can happen is that we're wrong."

Well, that seemed smart enough. I hadn't gone so far off my rocker that I wasn't able to hear some good old-fashioned logic. I took her swollen ankle into my hands, closed my eyes, and began saying a prayer. As I was praying, my fingers started moving over her leg out of my control. I kept my eyes closed the whole time. I allowed my fingers to be led. I pressed places in her calf, on the bottom of her foot, and by her toes. I don't know how long I had my hands around her ankle, but when I opened my eyes, the swelling had gone down completely and Light was able to walk with no pain.

"Sanka forta ienka danst." Good fortune has been done.

• • •

A director friend of mine invited me to his house for dinner. Ben was fantastic and funny and like a big cuddly bear. Going out in public was nothing less than frightening to me, but I figured I would trust Quiness that nothing was going to happen that wasn't safe. I showed up at Ben's house, got a quick tour, and we sat down to have an easy dinner together. I was relaxed and happy for the distraction. I wasn't getting messages or speaking funny at all and was glad about it. We were shootin' the shit like friends do when all of a sudden the shit started shootin' me. I began having visions of Ben and his wife sitting in the very places we were sitting having dinner.

"Does Jenny always sit here?" I asked, trying to be calm, having no idea what was going to come out of my mouth next.

"Yeah," Ben said. "Why do you ask?"

"Just wondering. I can kind of see her here." I had never met Jenny.

"Really? Like see her in the room?"

"Yeah. Sitting here talking to you." We were silent for a second, both of us smiling about Jenny. "She has a great energy."

"Oh, Jenny's the greatest. You two would like each other," he said. "You'll have to go out with us when she gets back in town."

"I'd love to," I said.

"You see things a lot, Anne?"

"Never before. But I am now, for some reason."

"What else do you see?"

I thought about it for a minute and began having images that I couldn't recognize. "I can't really tell," I said. "It's kind of unclear. And weird anyway. I don't want to freak you out, Ben."

"You're not freaking me out, Anne." I imagined that Ben had seen some pretty weird stuff in his life and nothing would probably faze him too much. "See anything now?" he asked playfully.

I wasn't about to tell him what I had been going through, but I was getting a strange rush all through my body and thought that if I explored the feeling, something fun might come of it.

"You sure I'm not freaking you out?"

"No. What?"

"Well . . ." I hesitated. "I'm not really sure what's going on right now, but I think my body might have something to tell me. Or you. I'm not sure which."

"Go for it," Ben said. I got the feeling that Ben was up for any kind of adventure. I got up from the chair and went over to where he had a rug in front of a window that led to a patio. I put my arms down at my sides and waited. "I have no idea what I'm doing, Ben."

"No problem," he said. "I got all night."

He waited and I waited and all of a sudden I had to sit down so I did, right there on the rug. And then it started coming to me.

"I think I'm being told about your birth, Ben."

"What?"

"I think I can see what happened to you when you were being born."

"You're kidding."

I wasn't kidding. It was all rushing through my body, as if I were actually going through Ben's birth process in my mind. As I was experiencing the sensation, I was telling him what I saw and how his birth would affect the course of his entire life.

"This is so amazing, Ben. Were you a breech baby?"

"God, yes. How do you know that?"

"I can feel it in my body. Do you see how I'm moving?" I was now lying down on the floor in a fetal position with my feet pushed out in front of me. I was moving my body as if I were experiencing the contractions as he had when his mother gave birth to him. When a contraction would stop in my body, my body would freeze, and I was able to tell him what information I had been given.

"You see, everything that happens to us in our life has already been determined before we come into this world, and we learn it as we are going through the birth process. Everything we feel or think will already have been programmed into our brains as we're coming out of the canal. Our birth teaches us so that we're not overwhelmed by our lives. We feel elation, suffocation, contraction . . ."

I went through another contraction. My body acted like an antenna for the information I was giving him. "We feel soothed, loved, choked . . . Fuck! This is so surreal, feeling this in my body right now."

"What does it feel like?"

"It feels like a smaller version of what your birth was. That's how I can tell you how you were born. I don't know how I'm doing this, I really don't."

"Tell me more. What else do you see?"

"You had a difficult birth. It was very painful for your mother. You heard her screaming and were scared that you were causing her pain, so you developed a high sensitivity to women and always relate to them tenderly. It was hard for you to relate to women sexually in high school and college because you always wanted to take care of them."

"Jesus, that's so true."

I experienced another contraction. I was now getting to the

point when his head was about to come out and was feeling choked around my neck. "I think your umbilical cord got wrapped around your neck, Ben."

"It did. My mother told me it did. Keep going."

"You were afraid to express yourself because of the trauma of not knowing what was going to happen to you. You felt choked, and because of this, you have always had a hard time expressing your feeling when with a woman. You take full responsibility for anything wrong and never want the woman to take any responsibility. Is that true, Ben?"

Ben told me it was true as he watched my body contract again. I could barely speak now.

"You have always wanted your mother not to feel guilty for what happened to you. She almost lost you, and you heard her screaming to get the cord off of your neck. You thought you did something to cause her all that pain, and you've been making up for it your whole life."

As I finished speaking, it felt like the cord was cut from around my neck, and I felt like I was pulled through a tight tunnel. My body fell limp on the floor. I was silent for a while and exhausted.

"Un-fucking-believable," Ben finally said.

"Fucking wild, Ben," I agreed. It *was* wild. Un-fucking-believably wild. I had never spoken to Ben about his birth, and unless he was completely bullshitting me, I knew how he was born and how it affected his life patterns with women.

"Are you okay?" Ben asked as he helped me rise and put his arms around me.

"Yeah. Are you?"

"Yeah. That was amazing to watch."

"I've never done anything like that in my life, Ben." We hugged and thanked each other for the experience.

"You wanna beer?" Ben asked.

"Please," I answered. "You sure you're not freaked out?"

"What's there to be freaked out about? It makes perfect sense." He handed me my beer.

"Cheers." We clanked glasses and went outside to stare at the moon.

• • •

Anna and I threw our arms around each other before I could even get out of the car. It had been a long time. I knew that I needed to spend the last of my twelve days with her. She had a house in the peaceful woods outside of Manhattan where she would hibernate when she wasn't working on the soap. We went inside and sat in the coziness of her eclectic log cabin, and I told her my tale. When I was finished she tucked me in bed and I slept for the first time in days. When I woke, I had stigmata on my feet.

I don't know why I even looked down at my feet in the first place. I didn't have a habit of checking out my body before getting out of bed, but something told me I must. In the center of each foot, I had what looked like a bloody, oozy scab. The holes weren't deep and they weren't bleeding, but they were identical in size and shape and looked like fairly fresh wounds. I was quite sure that Anna had not come up in the middle of the night and stabbed me with a screwdriver. But I was not sure at all what was happening to me.

I was beginning to feel like a freak. A loon. A crazy cartoon. Each day brought another weird occurrence more inexplicable than the day before, and this day was going to be no different. I didn't even believe in stigmata. I thought it was a Catholic thing. I carefully put on my socks and went outside to Anna's back porch. I wanted to be in the soothing breeze of the trees but was again thrown to my knees. Before I could scream, *I CAN'T TAKE IT ANYMORE* as loud as I wanted to, sounds started coming out of my mouth that could only be described as operatic. I was singing opera, or something like it. I went into a trancelike state for I don't know how long, then the opera stopped. When it was over, I fell on the porch weeping.

Anna had watched the whole thing and came rushing to my side. "What is wrong with me, Anna? What the fuck is *wrong* with me?"

"I don't know, sweetie. I don't know. Maybe there's nothing wrong with you. Maybe there's everything right with you."

"It can't be right. It's all too much, Anna. I had a vision last night that I was going to have the next Immaculate Conception. I can't take it anymore. I don't know what to believe and what not to believe. I'm singing fucking opera for God's sake, and I have holes in my feet that I didn't put there. I'm sick. Either I'm sick or I'm God, and I think I'd rather be sick. I hate fucking opera."

"Well, at least you're learning new talents."

I could always count on Anna for her sense of humor. She had tried to record my singing but—miraculously?—the tape recorder didn't record. It spun. The record light was blinking, but it did not record.

"I think I'm going to have a nervous breakdown."

"I think you already have."

CHAPTER FOURTEEN

VOLCANO

I was erupting. I had God coming out of my ears and movie roles coming out of my armpits. The race of Jesus versus the movie star was neck and neck. I returned from New York with a new fervor to become what God wanted me to become. I had Celestia watching over each move I made, and although I felt quite crazy, I decided to go with it. Other than checking myself into an institution, I didn't see any option. And who would believe me anyway? I was strong-bodied and healthy. Sure, I was having what some might call delusions of grandeur; I could have been labeled as some psychiatrist's textbook case, but how was I supposed to know that? I had never read Freud—I had never read much of anything for that matter. Besides, I wasn't roaming aimlessly through the streets unable to have normal conversations. I was perfectly normal.

No one in Los Angeles had any idea that I had completely split from myself and become another entity inside called Celestia. No one could tell from the way I walked or talked that I was from the fourth dimension. And certainly no one had any idea that I was getting messages from my planet every day about how to make the world a better place to live. From the looks of me, I was exactly the same as I had been before. Maybe I had a little less pain in my eyes. Maybe it looked like the therapy I had been doing had finally paid off. Maybe I looked like I was filled with love. And I was filled with love. Filled with love and lookin' to hand it out.

FRESNO, 2000

When I got out of the shower, I had no clean clothes. I wrapped a towel around me and called for the young girl.

"You don't by any chance have a T-shirt and some shorts I could borrow for our journey, do you? Mine are so utterly dirty."

She agreed and led me into a room with no furniture in it that I assumed was her bedroom. She opened a closet that was filled with only white T-shirts, all hanging in a row. She picked one randomly from the middle that had a picture of Mexico on it. Her brother handed me a pair of his shorts.

"Thank you so much."

On the floor she had three pairs of slippers. One pair was pink and shaped like bunnies and the other two were black and white like Mickey Mouse.

"Should we wear slippers to the ship?" I asked, liking that the slippers were so silly.

"It's too hot for me," she said. "But you can. Which ones do you like?"

I slipped on a pair of the mouse slippers and followed her into the living room, where a woman was now sitting on the sofa.

"This is my aunt," the girl explained. "She wanted to meet you."

As I was introducing myself to her aunt, I felt a tap on my shoulder. When I turned around the girl was holding a VCR tape of *Six*

Days Seven Nights in her hand. "Is this you?" she asked, pointing to my picture.

"That was me, yes."

"I've never seen the movie, no player," she explained. And I thought it was strange that she had a tape but no VCR. She pointed to her collection of tapes, all wrapped in their plastic casings.

"We'll get you a player in heaven," I said, "and then you can watch all the movies you want." Her aunt was staring at me sideways.

"I know this is kind of strange, me being here and all—" But before I could say more, the girl told me that her aunt spoke no English. "Tell your aunt that she is very beautiful and has healing hands." The girl did as I asked.

"She says her hands are too callused to be healing."

I looked at her aunt and smiled. "That's not true. She mustn't be afraid of her powers." I remembered the story of how Jesus had his feet washed when he went into homes. I thought I would return the favor.

"Do you have any cream? Hand cream perhaps?"

The girl nodded her head and went to fetch it. I knelt on the floor in front of her aunt and motioned for her to give me her hands. I felt how hard she had worked her whole life and wondered what she had done. Her hands were rough and cracked. When the girl returned, I put cream in my hands and slowly and softly massaged the cream into the woman's skin. When I was finished with her hands, I looked at her feet. They were bare and rough. They had walked many miles and served her well over the years, I thought. I touched her feet with the palms of my hands.

"You have worked so hard. You deserve to be loved and appreciated for your work." I took more cream in my hands and began massaging my love into her feet.

• • •

When I was asked to screen-test opposite Tommy Lee Jones for a movie called *Volcano,* I had to laugh. I had never been in an action movie before, and a blockbuster was way out of my league. I took it as a sign, and a not so subtle one, that I was on my way to making it big. Once I had erupted on the big screen, everyone would be interested in my message of love. I liked God and how clever his metaphors were and thought more about the Bible and all the metaphors in it: the burning bush, Daniel in the lions' den, Joseph and his Technicolor dream coat . . . Volcano . . .

I sidled myself right up next to the force called Tommy and had a blast at the audition. I pretended that I knew all about the earth and what was hidden inside its crevices. I spewed lines about tectonic plates and how they shifted. I must have done it like a pro because the next thing you know I was standing in front of sixteen cameras and getting paid for it.

But acting wasn't the only thing on my mind. My dream of directing was coming around the bend. I used all my time in between breaks on the set to polish my script and prepare to shoot *Stripping for Jesus.* I interviewed producers and cinematographers and got my cast ready. I was going to shoot the first week I was finished with *Volcano,* and there was a lot of work to be done. I had to make my movie for what was in my savings account, and that meant a lot of cutting corners and begging and borrowing. With the help of a spitfire producer named Effie Brown, I put my name on a letterhead and sent it all over town. We began asking anyone and everyone we knew for favors. I went to studios I had worked for and pleaded for their leftover unused film. I borrowed the house of a generous producer for the main set location. I hired designers and costumers who were hungry and wanted to make a statement. I cast actors who were my friends and would work for junk food and fun. I was working around the clock for the movie and around the clock for God.

Celestia was a ball of energy—better than any upper I knew. She was teaching me things left and right. I had one book filled and the other one was on its way. You see, when you're God you can do anything you want. You are everything. That's part of the message. To teach it, I had to learn it. I had every talent right at my fingertips, I was told. And, literally, my tips were teaching me. I would sit down with a pen and suddenly I could draw. And not just simple drawings, but intricate, detailed things like I had never seen before. I would get sensations in my left shoulder every time something new was about to come through my body. I would hold my hand in the air like an antenna and the information would come through. I wrote music and poetry; I saw visions of things that were going to happen in my future; I was able to channel dead people; I was taught to garden and told to plant trees; I was still doing healings and could focus in on another person's body like a laser to see their wounds. Each day I would be told I could do something new and would be led through the wheres and hows of it all. I felt like I could accomplish anything with Celestia inside me. And I did.

Volcano overshot by a week, the week I was supposed to shoot *Stripping*. Because we had all of our locations locked in and paid for, I had to start shooting the day *Volcano* wrapped. We had shot all night. I finished work at 5 A.M. and started shooting *Stripping* an hour later. I was the director, the star, and the coproducer. I sank every penny I had into the movie. It was *my* story. My life as I saw it, and I was determined to make it as good as possible. We had six days to shoot, and despite fires taking out our locations and camera crews not showing up and a drunken actor not knowing his lines and no money to pay anybody—we did it. And we had fun. Effie Brown is my hero. I've never seen anyone work so hard to make another person's dream come true. In one summer I had my first starring role and directed my first film. I was twenty-seven years old and completely out of my mind.

• • •

I needed normal, and I needed it bad. Feeling like I was superhuman was fun but becoming worrisome. I threw myself into editing and adopted a new mantra concerning the Celestia of it all: *Pretend that you're normal, Anne. Pretend she's not here, and she will disappear.*

"Anne, this is Bob. Bob, Anne. Anne, Dustin. Dustin—"

"Hi, Anne."

I could not believe the hands I was shaking. Who other than

God was allowed to be in a room with Bob De Niro, Dustin Hoffman, and Barry Levinson?

Pretend she's not here.

"Ahh . . . Barry? I think I got the wrong script here. It says I'm supposed to be reading the part of a man called Ames."

"No, you got the right one," Barry said. "I just want to see how the script reads with a girl in the third part. Don't change a line."

No way. I was going to be reading the third lead in a David Mamet screenplay? Who did I blow to get this gig? I sat down at a table with three of the most brilliant talents of our time and prayed that I would be good. Fuck good. I prayed I would be able to read. I had swirls in my tummy the size of the volcano that ate LA. It was just a reading, I had been told. No pressure, no audition. They didn't even know if they were going to do the movie. Just a reading. Just a listen and see.

I eked out the first line I had to read and wished I was reading the part of the waitress or "Woman on the Street #1," but no such luck. I was smack-dab in the center of all the action, buddying up with none other than Bobby D. and Dustin H. If that wasn't heaven, I didn't know what was.

Pretend that you're normal.

When I got the call that Barry had decided to go ahead and shoot this movie called *Wag the Dog* and that he was going to keep Ames a woman and keep *me* as Ames, I shot out of my chair like a clown from a cannon. My smile was so big I could have been a clown. I had more joy on my face than a kid with cotton candy and a pocketful of punch. It took quite a while for me to settle down and the reality to settle in, but it settled and settled hard. How the fuck am I going to act opposite the two greatest actors, *ever?* I felt sick to my stomach. When I arrived on the set I heard my mantra with a twist: *Pretend that it's normal. Pretend they're not there.*

Let me just say right here that I have never had so much fun in all my life. I feel honored and privileged that I got the chance to do that project. I was given the gift of a lifetime. I watched Barry tell a tale that would shock the world with its prescience, and I did it acting with none other than the best of the best. And speaking Mamet? Forget about it. As Dustin always said, "This is tougher than Shakespeare. This guy's a fucking genius."

Not a day on that set went by without me thanking my lucky stars. I learned more about politics and acting and directing in those six weeks than I have in my entire career. I gained confidence in my work that I hadn't had before and thought that with Celestia on my side, I just might attain my goals. Pretending that she didn't exist didn't make her go away. But she was always patient when I tried. I would sometimes play little games with myself and not talk to her for a couple of days and then, like I was sneaking around a corner, I'd say: "You there?"

Duh. Of course she was.

"Where do you think I went? I'm you." We'd have a giggle about the whole thing and get back to the lessons.

The main thing I was taught and would write about was love. *People are so confused over love and loving themselves and others. People are mean to each other and tease each other and discriminate against each other for no good reason. Power and greed and money are things that get in the way of love.* In the fourth dimension, which is where Celestia was from, there was no hatred. Everyone was equal there. There was no color, no race, and no creed distinction. In fact, there was no gender distinction. It was a world of Gods where everyone was everything that they wanted to be. There was complete acceptance and understanding there. I was going to bring the message from the fourth dimension to this world, and it went something like this:

Love is the understanding that all humanity deserves to have each and every one of their needs met with respect and honor and care. We can have complete love on earth—we just have to agree to it. All of us together have to agree.

Hate is an agreement we have made together. Hate is anything less than love. Hate is the belief that any one person is or deserves less than what any other person is or deserves.

Agreements can be changed—we just have to agree to change them. Change starts with yourself. We agree to not understand differences. We agree that we are right and those who do not believe as we do are wrong.

To change hate into love we must agree that all people are equal. All beliefs are worthy. All differences are beautiful. Anything other than that belief creates hate in ourselves.

We reflect the truth of what we believe through our actions. Our world is a collective reflection of those actions; we agree to war, to famine, to abuse. Each and every one of us plays a part.

If we believe anything less than love for everyone equally, we are agreeing to hate. Our world shows us just how deep and committed our agreement to hate is. Our agreement is ugly and nasty and bloody and brutal and we have all played our part by agreeing to less than love within ourselves.

Then it was Celestia's message. Now it's just what I believe.

• • •

If there were such a thing as a Hollywood Ball, it would be the *Vanity Fair* party the night of the Oscars. Everyone who is anyone is invited, and they all get dressed in gowns and tuxedos for the occasion. I chose a simple black ditty and threw on an emerald green velvet thrift-store coat so I didn't look like I was trying too hard. I didn't have enough money or care to hire a limousine for the occasion, so I jumped in my white, old-fashioned Toyota Land Cruiser and figured I would find a spot on the street and walk in without much fanfare.

Morton's is a Hollywood hot spot even when it's not hosting gala events, but this night is like no other. There are floral arrangements that would put any funeral to shame and a guest list brimming with fortune and fame. After saying hello to a couple of people I didn't know and attaching my hand to the closest alcoholic beverage in sight, I found myself bumping butts with a studio acquaintance of mine.

"You look lost!" she hollered over the din.

"I *am* lost! Help!" She slipped her arm through mine and agreed to be my escort through the sea of people I should have known or at least heard of.

"Who's that again?" I would ask when I saw a face that looked familiar.

"Did you grow up under a rock?"

"Kind of!"

"Tom Cruise, Anne. That's Tom Cruise." Not really, but almost. Even *I* would recognize Tom. We inched our way through the crowd, her telling the who's who of it all until my eye settled on one particular woman in blue standing across the room.

"Who's she?" I asked. My friend looked in the direction of where I was pointing,

"You've got to be kidding me, Anne."

"No, who is she?"

"That's Ellen DeGeneres. You don't know who Ellen DeGeneres is?"

I couldn't take my eyes off her. "I want to meet her," I said.

"You're in luck! I know her." My friend began me scooting toward the lovely lady in blue.

"You're not going to believe this," I said to Ellen after my friend introduced us, "but I saw you about a month ago outside of that store Maxfield's, and I was going to say something to you then, but I was too embarrassed."

"What were you going to say?" Ellen was curious. I was buzzing. I thought she was the most ravishing woman I had ever seen. She was standing there in a gorgeous ice blue suit and radiating such confidence and beauty, I knew I had to spend more time with her. I rambled off what I was going to tell her outside the store. "You see, three years ago a friend of mine took me to a Hollywood wrap party, and we were sitting in a couple of chairs people-watching when I noticed someone playing pool. I turned to my friend and told her that I was going to be in a relationship with that person someday. I didn't know what kind of relationship, but I was sure that we would meet, and I always trusted my instinct. My friend laughed and said, 'That's Ellen DeGeneres, the person whose wrap party this is. She has her own TV show.' Well, I was going to tell you that story outside Maxfield's, but I thought you would think I was a crazy stalker or something and even though I've never seen your show, which I'm embarrassed to admit, I always thought we would meet. So there you have it. It's nice to finally meet you. You look incredible."

"What a mouthful," she joked. She was funny, and I liked funny. "You didn't happen to be walking with a dog that day, did you?"

"I was! That's Sammy, my dog. We were going to the pet store down the street. Why?"

"Well, *you're* not going to believe this one. I was with my friend, and I saw you walking. I turned to him and said, 'Now, look at her. Why can't I meet someone like her?' "

"You're kidding me."

"I'm not."

"So we're supposed to go out or something," I said with a twinkle in my eye. "Why don't you give me your number, and I'll call you sometime?" I pulled out a pen and rested my napkin on her upper chest. "What's your number?"

"You better watch it. There's a guy from the press standing right behind me," she warned.

"What's that got to do with anything?" She explained that a big thing was happening on her show the next week. So big, in fact, she wondered why I didn't know about it.

"I'm coming out on national television. People are kind of interested to see who I'm spending my time with."

"Oh, I don't care about that." I readied the pen.

"Well, you should." She pushed the pen away.

"Why should I?"

She tried to explain that being gay in Hollywood was not something I wanted to be labeled as unless I was gay, and even then I might want to think twice.

"I don't care about all that labeling stuff, Ellen. Can I please have your number?" She gave it to me, but with a condition.

"Look, I'm not into straight women. I don't want to be an experiment for you."

"I totally understand and think you're even cooler for being so honest. I don't want an experiment, believe me."

I invited her to come with me to a place called Sky Bar where there was another Oscar party. She declined when I asked but was already there and waiting for me when I arrived. We talked all night in a cozy corner and never took our eyes off each other.

"I've never been with a woman before," I had to tell her. We were flirting up a storm, and I thought we might be falling in love. "But other than that tiny detail, I think we'll get along great."

Her manager offered to drive my truck up to her house so that we could ride in her limo together. I was fine with that, but told her that I had never left my dog alone and would be joining her only for a nightcap. When I leaned over to kiss her on the drive up to her house, it was clear that our sexual compatibility wouldn't be an issue. Our lips stayed locked until we were through her gate, up the drive, and face to face with her chauffeur who had opened the door. As we stepped out of the car I had to gasp.

"This is your house?" I stammered. "This cannot be your house."

"I'm glad you like it," she said, not comprehending what I meant.

"You don't understand. This is my dream house."

Ellen was confused. "You know this house?"

"Inside and out. My ex-boyfriend almost bought it for us to live in together."

It was too much of a coincidence for either of us to believe. Ellen had bought the house after Steve pulled his offer because I wasn't going to move in with him. She had heard the story about Steve but didn't know that I was the girlfriend. We both agreed it was a sign from God. We went inside and had the best night of lovemaking I had ever experienced.

"What are you thinking?" Ellen asked me after moments of silence lying naked in her bed.

"You sure you want to know?"

"I'm sure I want to know."

We were exhausted and staring at the ceiling. "I'm thinking that I love you."

"So why don't you marry me then?" We giggled at her response, not really understanding the seriousness of what she had said. In one night I had decided that I was in love. I had always heard of love at first sight. I had always fantasized it happening to me. Ellen fulfilled my fantasy.

Here was a person who was proud of herself and her sexuality. A person who didn't care what other people thought. A person who lived her truth and was telling it to the world. A person who was trying to help the world accept herself and her truth. A spiritual person, not a religious person. A person who cared for and appreciated my body and knew how to make me feel loved. A person I could communicate with. A person who made me feel seen and heard and safe. A person who happened to be a woman. I couldn't see it then, but I fell in love with a person who I thought was the exact opposite of my father.

You see, I had come to believe that if my father had been able to come out when he was younger, none of my abuse would have happened—because he would have been who he wanted to be. Ellen was who she wanted to be. Somehow I equated her being out about her sexuality with absolute safety for myself. I thought that with her I would have a lifetime guarantee that I would never be abused or hurt again. I decided that she was my knight in shiny blue armor and together we could teach the world to love.

• • •

"I can play this part with my eyes closed," I said to my agent.

"I know. It's you. Has you written all over it."

"It *is* me. I can nail this one, no problem."

"I think you can too." My agent always believed in me.

"Do they know who's playing the other part?"

"Sure do. You're not going to believe."

I thought the movie was a small, low-budget romantic comedy.

I got the comedy bug after doing *Wag* and thought a lighthearted romance would be fun.

"Harrison Ford."

"WHAT?"

"Can you believe it?"

"Can I believe it? No, I can't believe it! I'm never gonna get it now."

"You're a great actress, Anne."

"Fuck that! He's Harrison Ford! Why should he care whether I'm great or not. Fuck."

"Of course he cares."

"Okay, maybe he cares, but the studio won't. They're not going to hire *me* to play opposite *him*."

"You never know. You're hot right now."

"I'm not *movie star* hot. I'm not *Harrison Ford* hot."

"You never know." I liked his attitude.

"Who else are they looking at?"

"Everyone, Anne. Come on. It's Harrison Ford."

"That's my point. Shit! Do you think I can get a meeting?"

"What do you think I'm calling you for?"

"I got a meeting?"

"With Harrison and the director."

"*Me,* getting to meet Harrison Ford? Who cares if I get the part!"

"Get the part. I care."

"I care too, I guess. Fuck, man! Harrison Ford!"

I was standing next to Ivan Reitman, the director, when he walked in, all baggy-jeaned and casual.

"It is so fun to meet you, I can't even tell ya," I said.

"Nice to meet you too," Harrison said. I jutted out my hand. He shook and I shook harder, then he shook and I shook back. He was scruffy and unshaven and I liked that in a star. I liked that in a man. I guessed I wasn't the only woman who would like to be seeing Harrison in the flesh, let alone be shaking his hand. I guessed I was one lucky lady.

"You have no idea how lucky I feel right now. The first movie I ever saw was *Star Wars*. I wanted to fly with you in that ship." I guessed I wasn't the only woman that had ever told him that. "Oops," I said. "I don't mean to make you feel old or anything. I wasn't allowed to see a lot of movies when I was younger. I'm probably not that much younger than you."

"You probably are," Harrison said. "Let's not kid ourselves."

"Okay, let's not," I agreed. "I'm a lot younger than you, and I probably just blew all my chances of getting this role by admitting it, but who cares? I got to meet you and that's swell." Harrison and Ivan chuckled at me.

"You wanna read?" Ivan asked.

"Do I wanna read? Do I ever! Do you want to read with me, Harrison?"

"That's what I'm here for, Anne."

I was superglad they weren't asking me to leave. We sat down in two chairs that were set up for us in the little room. It wasn't that much different from my first soap opera audition, really, but I thought it best to keep that information to myself. This was a big movie audition, the biggest I had ever had, and I was tickled pink to be sitting where I was sitting—right next to the biggest movie star in the world.

We read some scenes off some sides, and I don't really remember how it went because I was too excited, to tell you the truth. I didn't really care about anything other than that I was there, meeting *the dude*. The night before I had met *the dame*. My life was swell, sweller than swell. My life was fucking awesome!

"How'd it go?" my agent asked.

"I don't know. I think he may have thought I was a dolt."

"A dolt?"

"I couldn't keep my mouth shut."

"Oh, Anne." I heard disappointment in his voice. I had a kind of reputation for saying what I felt without much edit in meetings, and he was afraid. "What'd you say this time?"

"I told him about *Star Wars*."

"Christ."

"I know."

"You didn't."

"I did. I couldn't help myself, I was too excited. I mean, it was so perfect—Ellen last night and Harrison today? It's too good to be true!"

There was a brief pause for a cough. "Sorry. What was that about Ellen?"

"Ellen! Oh, my God, I didn't tell you. I met Ellen DeGeneres last night, and I'm in love. I'm so in love! I've never had such great sex! No wonder lesbians are lesbians."

"Anne, take a breath."

"Okay." Breath. "What?"

"Let me get this straight. You slept with Ellen DeGeneres last night?"

"Yeah. She's amazing! She's gonna be my date for the *Volcano* premiere. Isn't that awesome?"

There was some more coughing, and I began to be concerned for my agent's health.

"Hello? Are you okay? Hello?"

• • •

I had a full day of press the day before the *Volcano* premiere and asked Ellen to join me and my "team" for lunch at the Four Seasons hotel. My agent, manager, and publicist would all be there, and I wanted them to meet her before the event. To go into the who said what of it all isn't really important. What is important is that my team sat Ellen and me down and, instead of the nice friendly lunch I had been looking forward to on my break, we were barraged with less than subtle opinions about the impending date to the premiere.

"You can't go with her. It'll ruin your career, Anne."

"This is everything we've worked for, you can't give up on it now."

"She's a woman—A WOMAN!"

"You've only been seeing each other for four days, FOUR DAYS!"

"Don't do this to yourself. You'll lose your next movie."

"You won't have a next movie!"

"The Harrison Ford movie won't give you the offer!"

"You'll be blacklisted!"

Hell and damnation to you both if you step foot in public together!

No client of ours licks pussy and lives to talk about it!

It was like a foreign press conference without the questions or the foreigners. It was an absolute nightmare. My "people" were telling me that if I took Ellen, the woman I was in love with, to the premiere of *Volcano,* I would lose my career. It was unfathomable and humiliating. It was scary and nauseating. I was angry, confused, frustrated—and sobbing. I had never heard of such absurdity in all my life. Who knew that my having sex with a woman would wreak such havoc on so many lives? Ellen was rightfully insulted and told me that she didn't want to ruin my career. She tried walking out of the room and my life right then and there. I dragged her back into the room and tried to get my life back into some perspective.

"What is going on here, folks? This is *my life.* My life is more important than a fucking movie, for crying out loud! I am in love with this woman, and it's about time you all wrapped your heads around that fact and stop being so petty! It's a *movie premiere*! For *Volcano*! Could we get a little *perspective* here? I am an actress! Who is going to give a shit about this? No wonder Ellen has to come out on national television—even you guys are scared of gay people."

My mind was reeling with the stupidity of it all. I had had no idea why gay people stayed in the closet, and now it was hitting me like a ton of bricks. People *want* them to.

"We don't care that you guys are dating, Anne. That's not what we're saying."

"It's not?"

"NO! We just think that you should wait until you've had a bit longer to see if this is really what you want for your life."

"I'm telling you this is what I want. You wouldn't be giving me the same advice if I was fucking a new guy, would you? Would you?"

"That's different. The world isn't ready for this."

"How do you know what the world is ready for? How is the world ready for anything when there are people like you making the decisions for them?"

I was so angry and confused. I had never experienced anything like this before and hated how it felt. I was overwhelmed and probably not as eloquent as I would like to have been in the room, but I had a new mission: *No one* was *ever* going to treat me or Ellen or anyone else the way I was being treated, if I could help it. I would go to the premiere and any other place I wanted with whomever I wanted. If a movie didn't want to hire me because of my choice to simply show up at a premiere with a babe, then I didn't want to work for those people anyway. Here Ellen had her coming-out episode about to air, she was on the cover of *Time* magazine, and everything she was trying to combat was being thrown in her face.

"Stay in the closet!"

"Be ashamed of who you are!"

"Don't go out in public!"

"Your love is bad love!"

Before we even stepped out of the limo together, Ellen was whisked away to the side of the red carpet to try to avoid anyone snapping a picture of the two of us together. Before the lights came up in the theater at the end of the movie, we were led out a side door, into our car, and told that we would not be going to the party because there would be too much press. I imagined the banner they might have hung on Ellen's front gate to congratulate me on my success: WELCOME TO DISCRIMINATION!

I didn't know what to do. Do I fire everybody on my team? Do I stand up and scream? Do I go on TV? Do I hide the real me? Do I have more sex? Which muscles should I flex? Do I ignore it for

today and hope it will go away? Do I pray to God above? My message is only love! *My message is only love!*

$$\bullet \quad \bullet \quad \bullet$$

Before either one of us had the chance to sip our coffee the next
morning, we were plastered on every cover of every newspaper all
over the world, with people waging bets on how long we would last.
Friends called me from different countries to see if it was true. There
was a huge price for any picture of the two of us together, and everyone and their brother tried to get the paycheck. There was a litany
of "I told you so" telephone calls and press statements from my
mother saying that I had entered into a sinful relationship. No one
could have prepared us for what was happening. Ellen had a better
idea than I that people would care, but even she wasn't prepared for
how much. I had been warned. But no one knew the extent of the
impact that we would have by simply showing up in public together.
We had no one to cling to, no one to get advice or support from
except each other, and we clung on like lovers on a sinking ship.
Without even knowing it, we were becoming one entity, joined at
the hip, and we hadn't been together a week. We were afraid to go
out of the house without the other. There were so many emotions
racing in each of us that we were afraid to be alone. We were afraid
to answer the phone.

As for my career? Who knew? Nothing could be predicted. I was
told that if *Volcano* failed at the box office, it would be my fault.
"How dare you steal the thunder by taking a woman to the premiere?" they screamed. "There's no way in hell that Disney will hire
you after what you've done!" It was like I had murdered someone
in my family. The pressure was so bad and the comments so ugly
that Ellen and I stayed holed up in her house for a week without
stepping outside the gate. I couldn't go to my house because there
was press camped outside my door. We were in shock. All we did
was fall in love, and not one person seemed to care how we might be
feeling. "Why can't they be happy for us? What have we done to
them?"

One day in the middle of the onslaught Ellen and I were sitting on the couch wondering what bomb would explode next when the phone rang. We listened for a while.

Ring!

"It's bound to be bad."

"Bound to be."

Ring!

"Should we even get it?"

"Probably not."

Ring!

"It can't get any worse."

"Don't be so sure."

Ring!

I picked up the phone. "Hello?"

"Anne?"

"Yeah?"

"This is Harrison." My heart sank.

"Hello, Harrison. How are you?"

"I'm fine. I bet you're not too good."

"Things have been better."

"Well, I'm just calling to say I'm sorry." My fear was confirmed. I knew I had lost the job.

"And, frankly, my dear, I don't give a shit who you're sleeping with. I'm looking forward to working with you. Try not to let this stuff get you down. It'll all wash over. It always does."

I couldn't believe my ears. There was actually one person on the planet that did not take my decision to sleep with a woman personally. "God bless you, Harrison." It was the first good news I had gotten since the premiere.

So my career wasn't in the toilet as had been predicted. For that I thank Harrison and Harrison only. I never found out the details about how I got the offer, but you can bet if Harry didn't want me on the picture, Harry wouldn't have had me. He will never know the gratitude I feel for his support.

Jesus and the movie star were in a tie game, but I had lost track of what I had been competing for in the first place. I was in a game I didn't know why I was playing. I was in a life I didn't know how to control. I was on the brink of insanity and didn't know how to get sane.

Help! Help! The sky is falling! The sky is falling!

CHAPTER FIFTEEN

THE HERO'S JOURNEY

I have come to believe that the insanity you are raised in becomes a part of you. In order to get the insanity completely out, you must equal it in your life so that you can get rid of it and move on. You don't get two cups of insanity and get to take only one cup out. At least I didn't. It's a terrifying thing to live through, and a blissful thing to be out of.

When you are a child of abuse and no one listens to you and no one confirms that you are being abused, you feel like you are insane. The more you are denied your reality, the more insane you get. I am a child of abuse. My abuse was denied my whole childhood. In order to survive the pain, I created a completely different world for myself. In my world I could fly down the steps away from my abuser. In my world there was love and no pain. In my world I loved everybody and everybody loved me. In my world there was no abuse given to anybody at any time. By the time I was an adult, the shame I had experienced had gotten so bad that I retreated to this world. This world became my reality. I called it the fourth dimension, and my name there was Celestia.

I believe that many people may think I went insane. I do not believe I am insane; I believe I went through a period of my life that was insane and it lasted thirty-one years. At the peak of my insanity I never knew what was going to happen to me next. I was constantly hiding and being asked to hide. It was confusing because I believed what was happening to me was really happening, but I knew that other people thought I was crazy. Hiding is never a solution. It works for a while, but then it all falls apart. By the time I finished shooting *Six Days Seven Nights* I felt like three completely different people, all existing at the same time. I was Anne-n-Ellen, the second half of the most famous gay couple in the world. I was Anne Heche, the closeted abuse victim with a burning desire to be a successful actress, writer, and director. And I was Celestia, a spirit being from the fourth dimension here to teach the world about love. The fight to keep all of me alive over the next three and a half years almost killed me.

• • •

The first year of Anne-n-Ellen was like a dream. We were like any other newly-in-love couple. We were out, gay, and merry. She came to visit me on my sets and I visited her on hers. We bought a house together and made it into a home we thought we would live in forever. We walked through rooms holding hands. We thanked God each night before we went to sleep and counted our blessings. Sure there were red flags, but we chose to ignore them. I focused on my fantasy of her, and she focused on her fantasy of me. We wanted to be the perfect couple. We didn't want the predictions to be right. We wanted to have perfect love. But no love is perfect when you aren't seeing the real person. We each had a person behind the curtain that came out in little bits, little arguments, but we didn't know what to do with what we saw. We didn't want to see reality. We had created a fortress of love for the whole world to see. If the curtains came down, we would be exposed in our vulnerability, in our imperfection. We were representing love for the gay community, we told ourselves. We had to be a united front.

But underneath the fanfare, there was the truth. When Ellen's show got canceled a year later, all the layers of lies we had built into armor began to be exposed. Ellen *did* care what people thought of her. In fact, she cared so much that the torture of the dropping ratings and the fear that she wouldn't work again started to consume her. She sank into a depression that would last the next two years of our relationship. She stopped having perspective. She stopped trusting that what she had done was a good thing. She began feeling like she was fighting the world rather than embracing a part of herself that she had hidden from the world. My fantasy about who she was to herself dissolved. Her fantasy of what it would be like to come out was over.

I saw the real Ellen and didn't know what to do for her. She was as vulnerable as I had been when we met. We both needed love and were destroyed by the thought that it might not be there. She wanted love from the world. I wanted love from my family. When I didn't get what I needed, I became Celestia. When she didn't get what she needed, she became a shell of herself, consumed by depression. Her feelings became so overwhelming that I didn't know where to put mine. My needs were not being met in our relationship, but I didn't feel like I could express them to her. I didn't feel my needs were as important as hers were. I was sorry for what had happened to her. I felt, as she did, that it was unfair, but I couldn't convince her that there was a positive side to all things and that she would get another show in time. I wanted to take care of her. I wanted her to know that she was loved, that the world did love her and everything was going to be okay. But nothing I said helped.

Ellen felt that there was no place for her in Hollywood anymore and wanted to move. She was feeling choked and suffocated and unappreciated. So we moved—out of a house we had bought together less than a year before. We isolated ourselves away in a bubble called Ojai and pretended that living away would make the pain go away. But the pain got deeper for both of us. I became focused on trying to make her life better and ignored mine. When I went away to do a movie, she became jealous and worried about me meeting someone else. Our arguments were brutal. She was terrified that I wanted to be with a man again. She didn't trust that I loved her and didn't care that she was a woman. So I stopped doing movies. I stopped doing anything that might make her feel insecure. She had a blanket of fear wrapped around her, and I adopted the blanket. We snuggled up next to each other and pretended for the world that we were fine.

It's amazing how productive you can become in a lie. I told myself it didn't matter that I wasn't acting anymore and focused only on my writing. I wrote two short films and three features in a year. Three of the projects were for Ellen to star in. I thought that if I gave her back a career, she would find herself again and we could return to being happy and in love. I thought if I loved her enough, she would then trust me and I could return to my acting. But I couldn't give her love for herself any more than I could give the world love for itself. I sold my shorts and directed them within a week of each other. I edited them at the same time and took a movie right after to pay the mortgage. My shield of workaholism was back and stronger than ever. I used my shield to ignore my feelings and told myself that I was doing it in the name of love. My pattern of abuse had returned. I was trying to be everything for someone else and lost myself in the process.

FRESNO, 2000

"Anne? Anne Heche?" I was still massaging the woman's feet when two cops came through the door.

"Yes," I said as I turned around. "How can I help you?"

"You *are* Anne Heche? Is that correct?"

"I *was* Anne, yes. Now I'm Celestia."

"Could you take your hands off that woman, please?"

"Certainly," I said. "I wasn't hurting her. You know that, right?"

"Could you stand up and put your hands behind your back?"

"Certainly I can." I slowly stood up and put my hands behind my back. "But I don't understand, Officer. What seems to be the problem?" As the officer cuffed my hands, I began to get afraid.

"Do you know where you are, Anne?"

"Yes, I know, Officer."

"Where are you? Could you tell me, please?"

"Certainly, I can. I am at this nice home where I am waiting for my spaceship. They have been lovely enough to host me until the arrival."

"Your spaceship?" The two officers looked at each other and sort of smiled. Then I understood and wasn't afraid anymore.

"Oh. You're here to help me board, aren't you? You are Peace and Calm, my escorts sent from heaven. It is very nice to meet you. I'm glad you have arrived."

"Would you have a seat over there, please?" He pointed to the couch and I happily obliged. I figured I had some more to learn before I got on the ship. Peace asked me all sorts of questions, kind of like a test, I assumed, to see if I was ready for the trip. I told him anything he wanted to know. I also told Calm about the directions back to my car. Calm took the piece of paper and headed out the door.

"Have you taken any drugs today, Anne?" I thought it was a trick that he was still calling me Anne.

"One pill," I said. "Is that enough?"

"Enough for what?"

"Enough for the ride?"

"And what ride is that?"

"The ride to heaven. I was told to take one before getting on the ship. I took it after my car stopped on the side of the road."

"You were told to take Ecstasy before getting on the ship?"

"That's right."

"What ship are you talking about?"

"The one that's going to take me to heaven. Do you want to come?"

"I'm not going anywhere, darlin'. You are."

"Why don't you come with me? You can, you know."

"I don't want to come with ya."

"Why not?"

"I got a family and friends. I'm fine just where I am."

"But they can all come too. Don't you want to live in a world of only love? Where there's no pain and no struggle and only peace?"

"If there's only peace, then I wouldn't have a job now, would I?"

"You wouldn't need one. Come on, Peace. Come. Please come to heaven." Calm arrived at the door with my car keys and a bag I had left in the car.

"It's here," he said, and I jumped to my feet.

"It's here? Is it time?" I searched out the window but saw no ship. There was a vehicle that looked very much like an ambulance.

"My ship isn't here?"

"No, ma'am. That's what I've been trying to tell ya."

And then it dawned on me. "It's coming someplace else and that thing's gonna take me?"

"You got it. That's gonna take you where you need to go."

"Oh, man. I can't believe I was wrong all this time. Leave it up to God to throw you for a loop." The young girl had been standing outside this whole time and was now in the living room holding a camera.

"Do you mind if I take a picture with you?" she asked.

"Sure," I said. I thought it was a good idea to remember this moment as well. Peace took off my cuffs and I took a picture with the girl and her family on the couch. Then Peace and Calm sat down on either side of me. When I had my arms around their shoulders and we were smiling nice and big, the girl snapped a picture.

"Perfect," I said. "Now I'm ready for the next stage of my journey."

• • •

It is not Ellen's fault that I didn't express my needs in our relationship. It's not her fault that I hid myself from her. We were in an ugly fantasy dance together. I think that if we had had the time in the beginning of our relationship to see each other for who we really were, we would have realized that we were very different people. Yes, we bonded over wanting to show the world that you can love whomever you want. But that bond was not enough to keep our relationship together. The fight that we fought side by side is one of the things I am most proud of in my life. I learned so much. I felt so much compassion. I heard so many stories and met so many wonderful people. I believe everything Ellen and I ever said and stood for.

Equal rights for all humanity is a constitutional right that is not upheld in our country and we pretend that it is. It is still illegal for gay couples to get married here, and that is a disgusting reality. We lie to ourselves every day that we are a country that accepts people for who they are. We lie that we embrace our differences. We do not now; we have not in our past. As long as there is a love between two human beings that is not acknowledged by the court of law, our Constitution is a lie. It does not say that all people are to be treated as equal except for gays when they want the right to get married like any other loving couple has the right to do. Our courts are a sham. We used to believe that blacks were lesser people than whites, and we made laws to justify our hatred. And still we have not learned from our horrid mistake and insult to a people. In California there are laws against gays getting married, and that was passed just last year. Yes, last year more than 50 percent of voters elected to treat one group of human beings with less respect and fewer legal rights than others. There is something terribly, terribly wrong here.

We participate in so many lies. Ellen and I tried to expose some of them by not lying about our love. It is hateful to ask someone to hide who she or he is. There are many people who try daily to fight the fight for human rights, and I applaud them. It is a hard fight. Mostly you are speaking to people who already believe what you do. When you go to schools or rallies you are preaching to the choir. And it's nice to feel heard; it's nice to feel a bond of vision for this world. But the most frustrating thing I learned in my journey is that you cannot teach people to love. To love another you must love yourself, and that is a furious battle that cannot be won until we all agree that we've lost it already.

We are not taught to love ourselves. How can we teach our children that the world is filled with love when we are also teaching them laws that clearly discriminate against another? Children know what they are learning. Children comprehend the lie. Why do you think kids kill each other in schools? Because they are taught every day by example that it is okay to hate. It is okay to battle someone for being who they are. We have wars—we have world leaders that tell our children through their actions that it is absolutely fine to fight and kill. Of course they think they can bring guns to school to solve their problems. It is absurd that we are continually shocked by it.

We don't even teach love like we teach sex education. Love has less weight than intercourse. We have classes to learn how to have safe sex, but we have nothing to teach us how to respect, care for, and honor our fellow human beings. Children are lost, and they are going to remain lost until we stop contradicting our own message. We are in a sewer of hate, and one person is not going to solve the problem. I wanted to be Jesus. I was willing to martyr myself for love. I stood up in front of almost a million people at the gay march on Washington last year and pleaded with them to love themselves. But what was I really doing? Pleading with my mother to love me.

Look at me, Mom. I am Jesus! See what I'm doing? I'm telling everyone that they are children of God! Isn't this what you wanted? Is this enough to get you to love me? Am I Jesus enough for you, Mom?

How can we learn to love ourselves if our parents are telling us through their actions that we are not worthy? Where do we learn? Who do we go to? It is so hard to figure out that instead we trust a lie that we're doing it already. Better to abide by someone else's law and another person's belief than do the work that needs to be done in ourselves to fix the problem. That's why there's religion. That's why there are gurus and goddesses and temples and statues. We want to believe that there is a better place than here, because here sucks. It's hard and ugly, and if we can believe that Jesus is going to come back and save us from it all, then we don't have to take responsibility for our part in the nightmare. Hell, yeah, I want heaven. The preachers and priests really did a number on us with that one. Sure, earth stinks, we know that. Tell us something we don't know. So then they tell us that we're here to suffer to get into heaven. Well, that sounds better. What do I have to do to get into heaven? Well, they say, just hand over some money and do a ritual and show up on Sundays and say your prayers. So we do. We get fed a bunch of malarkey that makes our heads spin so far around our brains that we can't make heads or tails of it. But we want to believe because we don't know what else to do. God saved Jonah; he can save me too. Sure, I'll say Amen. Sure, I'll take Communion. Sure, I'll go to confession. I'll do anything to take the responsibility off of me and put it on someone else. Hail Mary full of grace please send Jesus in my place.

• • •

I found myself face to face with the floor before I started to see that I had buried myself in my lie that I was okay. I had gotten so weak and so thin that I couldn't even stand up. I was so caught up in being Jesus and saving Ellen and the world that I forgot I was a human being.

It was the day that Ellen was shooting her first pilot after her show had gotten canceled. It had been three years. After the pilot she was going to go on tour with a comedy special she had written for HBO. She was coming back. It was everything I had hoped for for her. I had decided to shoot a documentary of her tour and was standing outside a film studio talking to people about getting some free film for our documentary when I felt light-headed. I left my director of photography with the people from Kodak and started inside to get some water. I didn't make it through the door. I blacked out. I was standing one second and lying facedown on the cement the next. The ambulance came and took me to the nearest hospital. All I could ask was whether or not I was going to live.

After I got some liquid in my veins, I told the doctor I needed to get to the studio where my girlfriend was shooting a pilot for her next season on television. I couldn't remember my name, but I could remember Ellen's show and that she was my girlfriend. The doctor released me from the hospital. I had broken my nose and had a severe concussion.

I showed up at the studio and pretended I was fine. Ellen knew something was wrong, but I told her it was nothing. As soon as her show was finished, my face basically exploded. I puffed out like a balloon. I had bruises and cuts from the fall, but somehow I kept the swelling down until I thought she could deal with the problem. Ellen checked me into the hospital the next day. I was there for a week, and no one could figure out what was wrong with me. I was gone. I was losing consciousness every hour. I didn't want to be here anymore. I had completely depleted myself of myself. I was lost. I needed help. I had needles in my arms feeding me food, and stickers and wires all over my chest tracking my heartbeat. Ellen wiped tears from her eyes as she stood by my bed, wondering if I would make it through the night.

FRESNO, 2000

"Anne? Anne?" I had given up on anyone calling me Celestia by this point. I was flat out and strapped on a gurney in an all-white, kind of cramped room that seemed less than glorious as a stopping point on my way toward heaven.

"Yes?"

"Good. You can hear me."

There was a man in a white coat with a pen in his pocket staring down at me. He looked kind of typically alien to me, and that made me relax.

"Yes, I can hear you. Who are you? What are you here to teach me?" I figured now that everyone I met was going to teach me something about how to take care of myself in flight or what to expect once I arrived.

"I'm a psychiatrist, Anne. Do you know where you are?"

"A psychiatrist, huh? Is this some kind of trick?"

"What kind of trick are you referring to?"

"You know, some kind of trick to see if I think I'm crazy."

"Do you think you're crazy?"

"No, I don't. Do *you*?"

"That's what I'm here to find out."

"Well, rest assured, Doctor. I'm not crazy, but it's nice of you to ask." He looked at the nurse and kind of rolled his eyes, which I thought was pretty weird for a doctor from heaven to do. It seemed sarcastic and unloving. I figured it was a test.

"I love you," I said. "Is this a test?"

"This is not a test, Anne." His voice was getting pretty stern now, and I didn't like the tone. "Do you know where you are?"

"Yes, I know. I told the nurse already, and I'm happy to tell you. But I know that you know that I know already. I'm at a stopping place where I am being prepared for the journey to heaven. All these questions are supposed to confuse me, but it's not working."

"You are in a hospital in Fresno, California, Anne."

"Well, if that's what you want to call it, Doctor, that's what I'll call it. I'm at a hospital in Fresno, California. I assume I am waiting for everyone to gather."

"Waiting for who to gather?"

"All the people who are going to come with me."

"Come with you?"

"To heaven. But you know all that already. You're here to test me to see if I know. Well, rest assured, I know. I know where I'm going. I know where you're from, and I'm looking forward to seeing it along with everyone else. How many are there?"

I figured the count would be high. I didn't understand the logistics of it all when I started out my day, but of course people would have to be told somehow. I wondered if it was going to be announced on TV or a loudspeaker or something: *SHE HAS ARRIVED! THE*

233

SPACESHIP IS ON ITS WAY. GATHER IN FRESNO JUST OFF THE FREEWAY!

"Do you know what year it is, Anne?"

"Surely I do. It's three thousand. Was that a trick too?"

"What. Year. Is. It. Anne?" He said it in a deeper tone, like that would scare me into saying something else.

I answered in a deeper tone to match his. "It. Is. Three. Thousand."

The doctor rolled his eyes again and left the room. I guessed I had passed the test and he was going to wrangle the people. The nurse was standing by my side and was kind of stroking my arm in a loving way. She was perfect and pretty.

"You're coming too, aren't you?"

"No, Anne. I'm not coming." Well, that made me tremendously sad. I loved my nurse an awful lot already. She had been so kind to me since I had come to the station.

"Why not? I sure want you to come."

"But I want to stay. I like it here."

"You *like* it here?"

She smiled so tenderly at me that I knew I should listen to every word she said. "Yes, I like it here. I have my family and friends here whom I love very much and who love me very much. I want to be here."

"You want to be here?"

"I want to be here."

This was a new concept for me. I closed my eyes and pondered the thought.

She wants to be here . . . wants to be here . . . want to be here . . .

• • •

When Ellen and I checked out of the hospital, I had a new lease on life, a second chance, if you will, to make my life what I wanted it to be. Honest and loving and healthy were the first things on my list. I was prepared to give my relationship with Ellen another chance. I was willing to give myself another chance at being up front about my needs and wants and desires. I wanted to have fun and think positively about our future together and the commitment we had made three years before. I would go on the road with Ellen, shoot the documentary as planned, and hope that our time on a bus for two months would bring us back together in a deeper and more loving way.

I started interviews for the crew I would take. I wanted it to be small. I wanted young, hungry people whom I would enjoy spending time with every day for twenty-four hours. I needed to keep the budget low and came up with an idea for the Internet to do weekly updates from the road. I learned new technologies that would help make the filming edgier and made agreements with companies to try out their equipment for small fees. Before we even hit the road I had raised a quarter-million dollars for the project, not including a private investor I had contacted who matched the money I was earning through the Internet project. It was exciting. I was on a roll. I was doing something I had never done before. I had a team of three talented young people who were going to come with me and teach me and learn from me all at the same time. YIPPEEE! It was more than I could have hoped for. Things were happy and life was good.

We hit the road the end of April and were planning to end the tour in New York, where Ellen was to shoot her HBO special. We started at the Equality Rocks concert the night before the gay march in Washington, D.C., and nearly died over the standing ovation Ellen got from the crowd of forty-five thousand people when she walked onstage at RFK Stadium. For about five minutes straight the audience went crazy for her. She was being appreciated in a way she hadn't been in three years, and she felt the love. We felt the love. Michelle, my director of photography, and Coleman, my cameraman, were shooting the entire time as the place roared with praise for their queen. Ellen was back. *Hurrah!*

The march the next day was a high point for us, there is no doubt. Ellen and I each spoke to almost a million people about love and acceptance, and we spoke with a fervor of activism in our voices as never before. When we were finished we climbed onto our bus with women cheering and pounding on the windshield: *Go, Ellen! Go, Anne! We love you! We love you!* I'd never seen such a thing. People were cheering for our message. People were cheering for us. It was scary and overwhelming and exhilarating.

I couldn't believe that people were cheering *my* name. *Anne, Anne! Look at me! Over here! Touch me! Anne! Anne!* If ever there was a Jesus moment, it was then. They were screaming for me to touch their hands. What I had said meant something. And I was honored. I was touched. I was pleased with what I had said and proud of what it meant. But I didn't know then that my message was for *me,* not them. I had used the platform to tell myself what I needed to learn.

Be who you are. Tell all of your truth. Stand up for yourself, no matter how hard it may be. Pure love awaits you when you are completely honest with yourself. Your path is your own. No one can tell you what to do or how to get there. Be strong. Be brave. Listen to your heart.

After only a couple of weeks on the road Ellen and I got into a routine with each other that was damaging to both of us. Yes, the trip was grueling, but that wasn't what the problem was. I was beginning to look at things differently since the hospital. I wanted to see clearly and truthfully if we loved each other, or loved an *idea* of each other. I was afraid it was the latter. I did anything I could to keep the truth away. I stood by the side of the stage every night and watched her show over and over again and cheered for the woman whom I had fallen in love with. I tried to get pregnant, thinking that if we started a family, our internal relationship problems would go away. But that was just another cockamamy scheme to try to fix something that was broken.

I didn't want the isolated life we had created for ourselves. We had stopped having fun together. We barely had any friends. Our life had become one long note of trying to save the world, and it was apparent each night that Ellen and I were growing apart in our convictions and our needs.

I took a small role in a movie, which was going to shoot while the tour was on a break, called *Prozac Nation.* In my time away I found that I had been ignoring myself too much. I wanted other things for my life than I was able to have in my relationship. I loved my acting. I was starting to love myself. My dreams and goals were surfacing again—and they were for me, not Ellen.

I came up with an idea to write a book while I was doing yoga one night. I was ready to face my abuse and get out of my abusive patterns once and for all. I started writing on my breaks on the set. As the truth about my life fell onto the page, I realized that I had been doing the same thing I had always done: trying to adapt my life to accommodate others.

By the time we got off the tour, I was ready to face the real me, and the real me had some problems. One of them was my relationship. I asked Ellen for some space to figure myself out. I needed friends, I told her, and a place for an office where I could think and write outside of our house. It was an ultimatum, as she pointed out. If I didn't get those things, I was going to leave her.

"I don't want a girlfriend who wants those things."

She said it simply and calmly. It was her right to have what she wanted in a relationship. It was my right to leave. I packed a bag, walked out the door, and never went back.

FRESNO, 2000

"Your friends are on their way, Anne," the nurse's sweet voice was whispering in my ear.

"They are? Oh, my God. I'm so excited. They're coming. They're coming with me."

"No, Anne. They're coming to take you home."

"Take me home? My home in heaven?"

"Your home in Los Angeles."

"I can't go there. I can't go back there. I can't go back." Fear was rushing through my body. "What about my ship? I have to get on my ship."

"There is no ship, Anne. You're going to go home."

Tears started streaming down my face. I was panic-stricken. I didn't understand. "What about heaven? What about going to my home in heaven?"

The door opened and I saw my best friend, Kathy, coming to my side. She took my hand. "Hello, sweetie," she said. "How ya doin'?"

The nurse shut the door behind her, leaving us alone to talk.

"Oh, Kathy. I was going to go to heaven. My ship was going to come and take me to a place where there was love—all love, Kathy! And I thought you would come with me. I thought you and Lauren would come. Don't you want to come to heaven, Kath? Isn't there a ship that's going to come and take me there?"

"No, sweetie. There's no ship. We live here. We want to live here."

"But it's so hard and so painful, Kath. It hurts so bad and love is so hard to find."

"Love is hard to find, yes. But we found each other, didn't we? I love you, sweetie. I love you, and I want you to stay here so I can keep loving you. I don't want you to go away." Her words were so tender and filled with truth.

"Oh, Kathy. Oh, Kathy, what have I done?" I was scared and crying. I knew that my dream of my ship was lost. "My ship isn't coming, is it?"

"No, honey. There is no ship."

"And I'm not going away, am I?"

"I'd rather you stay," she said.

"But it's so hard to be here."

"It's hard to be here, yes."

It was all hitting me now. The reality was sinking in that I wasn't leaving, but I didn't know why I had thought I was. "What have I done? Where did this all come from?"

"I think you've had a lot of pain in your life that you focused outside of yourself and that's what you're seeing now."

"The fourth dimension. I created a fourth dimension. I was going to go there for good."

"I know, sweetie. I think it has to do with your abuse. I think it's time for you to connect what happened to you as a child with the world you created." As she said the words, it all started to make sense to me.

"I created the world so I could escape the pain."

The realization was overwhelming. I had lived with so much fantasy in my head for so long, and in a moment's time I was seeing the truth. "Does this make me crazy? Am I crazy, Kathy?"

"I don't think you're crazy, Anne. I think you're a survivor."

My whole life became clear through the bleariness of my tears. I had created the fourth dimension and Celestia from the time I was a little girl. As I grew up, so did the world. At first I could fly. Then I could heal. "People will believe anything they want to believe," God had said to me. I needed to believe so that I could get out. With my friend by my side, I realized that I wanted back in.

"I was so lonely, Kathy. I was alone when I was a child, and I was alone going to heaven."

"It's no fun to be alone."

"It's no fun to be alone."

"I want you to stay here."

"I want to be here."

For the first time in my life, I understood my insanity. With the help of my friend I was able to give it away. I wept out my fantasy world onto Kathy's shoulder and breathed in the world of love she was giving me with her embrace. After thirty-one years of flying through space, I had landed and was finally home.

EPILOGUE

·

LOVE/THE OTHER SIDE

When I woke up the next morning, I looked like I had been through the rinse and spin cycle in a human washing machine. I had sweated so much in the night that I soaked through a hospital gown and the gurney's sheets. There could have been puddles of me on the floor. When your mind cleanses, your body cleanses. Out with the old and in with the new. You know that Doublemint gum commercial where there are "Two—Two—TWO mints in one"? Well, I was like "Three—Three—THREE chicks in one." I could tell I was back, I was present, I was with myself in myself. The best way to describe the feeling is sane. I felt *sane*. I looked at myself in the mirror and saw me. Not the me that should've looked better or the me that was God, or the me that was anything other than Anne. I was just Anne. Messed-up and ugly and war-wounded and proud. I knew I'd won the battle. I knew I was on the other side. And not by accident. I had made a choice. I chose to be sane. I wanted to be here on the earth because I liked it here. Reality was better. For the first time in my life, I knew that reality was better. Now all I had to do was convince *them*!

Somewhere in the night my manager—who also happens to be my other best friend, Lauren—had arrived from Vancouver where she was shooting a movie. I don't know what was said on the phone to get her to fly down and see me, but it must've been something like: "Holy fuck, Anne has gone fucking crazy in Fresno, and you have to come down."

She joined Kathy and another dear, dear friend and business manager, Harley, who had already arrived at the hospital to confront the disaster. The thought was that I had had a psychotic break. *A psychotic break,* Jesus! That's bad, really, really bad. The doctors were considering putting me into a mental institution as my three friends tried to convince them of my impending sanity: "Surely she'll be sane tomorrow, Doctors. She's never gone nuts before."

I'm kidding. They were scared, worried, concerned, and freaked-out, to name only a few of their emotions. Lauren and Kathy had been aware of Celestia, but only little bits of her, and they certainly weren't going to tell the doctors anything that would tip the scales toward a psych-ward stay. I'm sure there were discussions of what I might have ingested, and there was probably a drug search to see if I should be thrown in jail. I could hear them all talking and debating through the doors. It's funny—when they think you're crazy, they also think you're deaf. The race of Jesus versus the movie star was over, and I had been dumped at the finish line with no fourth dimension in sight. Psych ward or prison. Psych ward/prison. Psych ward/prison. These were not the options I had in mind.

Where I would have called these earth-angels fighting my fate saints or kings in the past, I was now absorbing the reality that there were people in my life who cared deeply for me, and they were called friends. I was in trouble and they came to my rescue. Within minutes of being called, all three hopped on the first flights they could to

get to my side. As I sat up on my gurney that morning I was con-
fronted with the first gift one arrives with on this planet—love. Love
of friends. Real love, not fantasy love, just love. As I tried to put into
words the experience I had had the day before and the necessity of
the release I had to experience, they listened and understood. I had
had to do what I had done. There was no place else for me to go
except to see my fantasy all the way through. I needed to see this
fourth dimension that I had clung to my whole life. I needed to confront the fact that I was not Jesus or Celestia or any-other-fucking-
body. If I didn't go all the way, I would not have been able to get
rid of it once and for all. I had thought my fantasy world was safe.
My whole life I had escaped to there to be safe. I needed to see that
it wasn't. It was, in fact, a lonely place that I would retreat to when
I was scared and being abused. I wasn't being abused anymore. I had
friends, my chosen family, and neither they nor anyone was going to
hurt me anymore. Had I not gone to Fresno that day, had I not taken
the fantasy down the long road to its conclusion, I never would have
known that there was an end.

Somehow they convinced the doctors to give me a sort of mental
test to show that I was able of mind and sound of body. I was asked
the questions I had been asked the night before, and this time I
had the right answers.

"Do you know your name?"

"My name is Anne."

"Do you know your last name, Anne?"

"Heche. My name is Anne Celeste Heche."

"Do you know where you are, Anne?"

"I am in a hospital in Fresno, California."

"Do you know what year it is?"

"It is the year two thousand."

My friends waited with bated breath as I answered all the questions correctly.

"I'm going to release you now, Anne. You can go home with your
friends." Wow. Relief. Joy. Each and every person in that hospital
took such good care of me. They held my hand and told me the

truth. I will never be able to repay them for the stability they offered as I battled my demons in front of them. Their hope for my return to sanity was present in my room, and I must have felt its power. I could not have gone through what I went through without them.

The next fiasco was getting me out of the hospital without anyone noticing. The press had gotten wind of my arrival, and they were waiting outside each of the sliding-glass exit doors. Of course they knew. How couldn't they know? Some famous chick had been wandering through fields of dirt with her shirt off, asking people to join her on her spaceship to heaven. Even I would want that story. Kathy had brought me some clothes, and I donned a floppy cap and black glasses for my escape into the real world. I was the opposite image of glamour. I looked like a sewage rat in a human's clothes lookin' to take a stroll on the beach. I stumbled into my truck, which Harley had rescued from the side of the road the night before, and we sped off into the sun-filled Fresno skies, hoping never to return. Yooowwwzzzieeeeee! It's a doozie goin' crazy! It's a thrill to be sane.

Thank you, Fresno. Thank you, every single person who helped me that day. I thought you were there to teach me about my future, and I was right. There was just a little mix-up about my destination. With gracious and loving hands you all delivered me safely into the arms of planet earth. I am eternally grateful that you knew where I belonged even when I didn't.

· · ·

The press had a field day with this one. And why wouldn't they? "Famous Gay Actress Breaks It Off with Girlfriend and Goes Crazy in Fresno." They compared me to every other person who had gotten caught doing something weird in a stranger's backyard. And who could blame them? It was strange. I had never done anything stranger, at least not that anyone had heard of. There was nothing to deny, there was nothing to say in my defense. It was true. Funny that. When something's true, what can you do? I was all over the news for the next two weeks. I was the butt of everyone's jokes from Leno to Letterman. I deserved it. Sure, I would have liked to have had my epiphany in the privacy of my own home, but part of my problem was that I had kept private for too long. My insanity was big. It was huge. So I came out about it in a huge way, there is no question about it. Am I proud of it? No. Am I glad about it? Yes. When you hide, you will find a way to get unhid, if that is what your goal is.

• • •

I had walked into a therapist's office when I was eighteen years old because I knew I had some problems. For the next thirteen years of my life, my number-one goal was to get over my problems and live clean, on my own terms, without the shit and shame of my past. Not one day went by when I was not doing something to get my abuse out of me. If I wasn't in therapy, I was writing scripts. By twenty-five I had written and directed a play about abuse. By twenty-seven I had written and directed my first movie about it. I am now thirty-one and I have written a book about it. I'm done with the topic. I had a mission. I was committed, and I will tell you the freedom is WORTH IT. That's why I wrote this book. I wanted to be free. For me. Not anyone else. Yes, I hope it helps. I hope people see how bad it can get when you live in a lie. I hope that people get the courage to talk about their abuse before they find themselves wandering through dark caves of insanity and into the homes of strangers seeking God. I hope that parents and teachers look at signs and listen to their children when they tell you their truths. I don't believe that a child can make up the kind of shit that happened to me. Abuse is an ugly truth and it is in this world and it happens to a lot of kids in this world. Sure, I'd like it all to be exposed and go away for good, but that's not why I wrote this book—and I couldn't do it even if I tried. I wrote this book to say good-bye once and for all to my story of shit and shame and embrace my life choice of love. The fact that there are people reading my story is the icing on the most beautiful cake in the world that I imagine says HAPPY FREEDOM, ANNE. YOU HAVE MADE IT TO THE OTHER SIDE.

I have a boyfriend now whose name is Coleman. He is the most loving and giving and special person I have ever met. He has taught me what it is like to be in a loving relationship that is of this earth. He has allowed me to embrace all of my past and see myself as a human being who survived a life that was hard and did it the only way I knew how. I didn't do it perfectly. I made a lot of mistakes. I hurt a lot of people. There were moments writing this book when I was so ashamed of the things I had done that I didn't think I could continue. If it weren't for his encouragement and constant support, I would not have been able to. I wish a Coley for everyone when they leave their shit and shame behind. But there's only one of him, so you'll have to find your own.

I'm so corny at heart. I want the best for everybody. I really do. I wish there was no pain, but I know it's out there. I wish there was only love, but I know there's hate. I know we have shields and armor to protect ourselves because the journey is hard. I give you all my love and support on your journey. I hope you find happiness and love and peace because it is your right to have it. You are children of human-ity and you deserve to have all your needs met with honor, respect, and care.

So I am wishing you love. Love that embraces you for who you are. Love that sees all of you and asks no sacrifice. Love that you can accept because you have loved yourself first.

ACKNOWLEDGMENTS

Without the belief of Lauren Lloyd, my manager and soul sister; Steve Dontanville, my incredible agent and friend; Joni Evans, my champion and guide; Lisa Drew, my editor and teacher; Emily Remes, my ass saver; Kathy Greenberg, my spirit mate and confidante; Lisa, my light; and Coleman Laffoon, my partner and love, I would not have been able to write this book. I want to thank everyone at Scribner who worked so very hard to make this book a reality. Your diligence and support is astounding. I would also like to thank Dr. Frawley-O'Dea, Gloria Steinem, and Anne Lee for their support and encouragement and my continuing education.

CREDITS